TEACH ‎ F

pu ‎ ‎ *relations*

J Harvey Smith

Hodder & Stoughton

A MEMBER OF THE HODDER HEADLINE GROUP

British Library Cataloguing in Publication Data
A CIP catalogue record for this book is
available from the British Library

ISBN 0-340-60752-1

First published 1995
Impression number 10 9 8 7 6 5 4 3 2 1
Year   1999 1998 1997 1996 1995

Typeset by Rowland Phototypesetting Limited, Bury St Edmunds, Suffolk.
Printed in Great Britain for Hodder & Stoughton educational,
a division of Hodder Headline Plc, 338 Euston Road,
London NW1 3BH by Cox and Wyman Ltd, Cardiff Road, Reading.

CONTENTS

—————————— **APPENDICES** ——————————

ACKNOWLEDGEMENTS

To the many editions by Herbert Lloyd – and later, Herbert Lloyd and Peter Lloyd – that preceded this one in the *Teach Yourself* series, apologies that it has turned out rather different: but that's the times we live in. My thanks are due to Dr Jon White for his initial encouragement and for reading the text; to Danny Moss for suggestions on its organisation; to Paul Attenborough for his interest, constructive criticism of the text and offers of source material; to the Institute of Public Relations (IPR) for permission to draw freely from its publications; to Infopress for asking several of its staff to record a day's work in a PR consultancy; to the 1994 IPR president Mike Beard of Taylor Woodrow for similar cooperation for a corporate PR department; to Smythe Dorward Lambert and the Centre for Communication Studies for early access to their research into the new technologies and internal communication, and communication training for management; to Paul Noble of Bournemouth University for help with academic and student material; Leeds Metropolitan University; Stirling University and West Herts College, Watford; and to George Gaskell and Rob Briner, speakers (with Jon White) on the IPR Mind Link lecture programmes on psychology.

– ABOUT THE AUTHOR –

J Harvey Smith is editor of the Institute of Public Relations Journal and an independent public relations consultant. He is a history graduate of St John's College, Cambridge, and holds the Communication, Advertising and Marketing Education Foundation Diploma in Public Relations. He is also a Fellow of the Institute of Public Relations and a member of BAIE Communicators in Business. In 1993, he won the IPR's PR Means Business competition, held in Surrey, Sussex and Kent.

── INTRODUCTION ──

I have tried to make this book easy to read for anyone who chooses to gallop through it from start to finish. At the same time I have tried to construct it so that chapters are useful, self-contained reference material when read on their own. I have made no attempt to be exhaustive because, for a short book, that would mean hundreds of thin entries leading nowhere. Similarly I rejected the tempting format of covering all the different work sectors of public relations practice (financial, local government, voluntary organisations, crisis management and so on). Such specialist knowledge is outside the book's purpose. Instead I have chosen to explore the general ideas behind drawing up a public relations programme, and to look at some of the knowledge and skills needed. To convey an idea of the realities of the work I have punctuated the text with a few simplified case study examples, as well as offering longer studies in the chapter on campaigns. In the same spirit, I have included one or two personal work diaries in the chapters on corporate communications and careers in PR.

To teach yourself public relations you have to explore two levels simultaneously: strategy and planning; as well as technical operations like a press conference or taking part in an exhibition. Yet when you begin work in public relations you will usually be employed for your technical and legwork abilities. So you may worry that your strategic brain will be in danger of falling into disuse. Chapters 2 to 6 attempt to equip you for both. Also, be assured that strategic understanding is necessary to carry out all but the most mundane of PR tasks.

I have treated three subjects at what might seem disproportionate length. Good writing, because of all the forces aligned against it. Psychology, because many academics regard its ideas as underpinning public relations practice in affecting attitudes and changing behaviour, yet it is little covered in heavier PR text books. Finally, the new technologies, also highly relevant of course in external relations, are the basis of the section on internal relations in Chapter 3.

The biggest change in public relations education in the 1990s has been the creation of numerous university level courses. In August 1994 the Vocational Guidance Association listed public relations as the second most popular career, behind marketing. Business, pressured by environmental demands on the one hand and organisational change on the other, is realising that its young managers will benefit from understanding public relations thinking. Meanwhile, those new technologies are pushing communication needs to the fore.

I hope that *Teach Yourself Public Relations* may help sixth formers and school leavers, first year PR students, the directors of small businesses, young managers in big business, and anyone who needs to know more about public relations in the 1990s. That's everyone, isn't it?

J Harvey Smith 1995

1

DISCOVER PUBLIC ——— RELATIONS ———

1.1 Reputation, perceptions and relationships

What do you think public relations is? You are unlikely to know much about other topics in the Teach Yourself series – linguistics, say, or croquet – before reading about them. But you will almost certainly have a view on public relations (its reputation travels ahead of it in the media). You may think it is about getting coverage in newspapers and magazines, on radio and television. It is, but not only that. You may think it is holding a conference or seminar, having a stand at an exhibition, making a video. Indeed, they may be part of it. You may think that public relations is about how organisations work out ways of causing the least offence to the environment and society, while still managing to stay in business. Or you may realise that all organisations depend to some degree upon other groups: suppliers, employees, government, civil servants, pressure groups, local authorities, customers, the media, the general public, even upon individuals.

These are some of the 'publics' that are the concern of anyone practising public relations. Every organisation enjoys, or suffers, relationships with its publics that continually affect its own well-being – and that of its publics. These relationships are not necessarily chosen. They exist whether you like it or not. Locate a factory and it will have a surrounding community that may object to noise, smell, emissions, working hours, trucks. The local MP needs to know about it; the local authority will have to give permission; Friends of the Earth may not like the product. Nowadays these publics cannot be ignored.

How does this simple idea fit in with what you thought public relations was before you read these paragraphs? How important do you think that makes the job of public relations, of having good public relations? In teaching yourself about public relations it is important to clear out of your mind any impressions that you may have picked up from references in the media or in casual conversation. Start from the point that public relations is everything to do with an organisation's relationships and therefore with its reputation.

When one person has a relationship with another it is essentially for its own sake. You may have to nurture it but you just want it to be. The best, the lasting relationships, are not exploitative. It is less so in business and commerce. Organisations are set up for a purpose. Companies make profits by providing services and producing things. They want to sell these so they can grow, expand, make more money. Other organisations have different purposes: charities raise money for causes; trade associations look after the interests of their members; pressure groups try to change the world; a stamp club wants to give its members pleasure and information. All look at the world from their own point of view and many want the world to adopt their point of view.

As they go about their work these groups form, or find they have, or need, relationships with other groups. A gun to the head is a form of communication (but bad public relations). However, people will also try to do what you want if they know you well and want the relationship with you to continue. Or if they can have something in return. Or if your argument is convincing. Relationships condition actions and reactions. They set you thinking: how should I approach this, when would be a good time, will I harm the relationship? Does it matter?

Conversely, the more power an organisation has, the less it thinks it needs relationships. But the poorer its relationships the harder it will be to keep its power in the longer term. Its enemies may build relationships that weaken it.

Perceptions and impressions

Public relations works at two levels. First, at the general level of public perception. All individual publics read, watch or listen to the media. They form impressions of what an organisation or an individual seems to be like and develop fixed ideas even though they have no direct, personal contact. Merv Hughes, the Australian fast bowler, said after the 1993 Test series: 'It's up to the media what people think of you, and the media has been very kind to me.' He said he liked the English crowds, the chants of 'Sumo' and the fake moustaches. Equally, pop stars and celebrities cultivate a public persona that may have little to do with what they are like in private.

The second level is your own direct experience of an organisation. Take as you find. PR needs the media but is careful of it, mainly because of the fear that messages will be distorted. So it moves to ways of communicating directly, not indirectly. Don't let someone else tell your story is the first rule of selling. Often, the private knowledge and the public persona may clash. You might say: 'What good public relations they have. No one would know what bastards they really are.' Or: 'I thought you were good people to deal with but what I read in the trade press shows I was wrong. We are choosing another supplier.'

If you are an employee you will almost certainly know what the company you work for is really like – and it may not be how their reputation is projected in the media. Messages need to be consistent. One of the reasons for the concerted efforts companies are making in the 1990s at internal relations and employee communication is motivation. But another is to avoid a contradiction between a company's public relations' stance and what employees say about it in the pub.

Competing aims

It would be a better world if we were all more altruistic. That human quality survives only thinly in the 1990s and is characteristic, mainly, of deeper personal relationships. Commercial organisations do everything to get what they want. That is, a world ordered in a way that makes them successful, achieves their objectives. They are in competition, however, with others like themselves. This means that there are thousands of silent wars going on in which public relations and reputation are part of the firepower. If a competitor's business fails it is only a bad thing if it happens to be bad for the market as a whole. Otherwise there will be new business to compete for, able employees to recruit, cheap equipment to pick up. If a company is in fact ruthless but is popularly thought of as a worthy contributor to society, why should it alter its public relations?

Non-commercial organisations may seem different but each is still pursuing its own purpose, defending its own corner, standing up for what it believes in – whether or not fighting heart disease is a better purpose than selling shoes, working for a greener future more creditable than making bullets. Both types of organisation will put their public relations resources to work in favour of their discrete aims.

If it's familiar, it's favourable

It is this partiality which brings down the wrath of journalism on public relations practitioners ('they would say that, wouldn't they?') The general public are less vociferous. Most of the time they do not see what goes on behind the scenes: business dramas of which the journalist catches glimpses from the wings.

The general public tends to follow the familiarity-favourability 'rule' which shows up in MORI (Market and Opinion Research International) research. MORI monitors attitudes, plotting familiarity against favourability. Usually when you are familiar with a business sector you tend to think about it favourably. If you are unfamiliar with it you think about it unfavourably. For instance, polls of so-called Captains of Industry (the business leaders of the top 500 companies) have shown they are very familiar with private health care, accounting and information technology and regard them highly. Public relations, on the other hand, consistently bucks this theory: Captains of Industry are equally familiar with PR but do not regard it very highly. Management consultants have come off even worse in some studies.

PR is misunderstood

The feeling within the PR business is that neither journalists nor business leaders really understand what public relations is. It is an irony they have lived with for a long time and stems from the multiple nature of public relations.

As a strategic force it is often unseen. The part it plays in deciding the essence of a firm or product, in planning, and in the conscience of industry, is out of the public eye. The presentation aspects of public relations, especially the stunts, the hype, the stagey photo-opportunities, are seen all the time and taken to be all public relations is. That and the everlasting search for media mentions and sound bites.

Accusations of superficiality also arise when instead of tackling root causes, public relations experts are called on to cover up, distract attention, neutralise criticism. These are the notorious 'public relations exercises'.

The profession has the task of demonstrating that good public relations is not shallow, superficial, cosmetic but is fundamental to the well-being of organisations.

1.2 Definitions

In the early days of public relations, the American Edward Bernays, regarded now as the 'father of public relations' (he was 103 in 1994), used the term 'engineering consent'. The Institute of Public Relations (IPR) avoided the manipulative undertones in its 1948 definition (mildly amended in 1987) to concentrate on the idea of 'mutual understanding': 'Public relations practice is the planned and sustained effort to establish and maintain goodwill and mutual understanding between an organisation and its publics.' Quentin Bell, a public relations consultant, does not see his company selling mutual understanding but, rather, persuasion. Warren Newman, director of corporate relations at General Utilities and previously with AEA Technology (nuclear fuels) believes acceptance is sometimes as much as one can hope for.

Organisations try to sustain or change relationships with two aims in mind. The first is that they understand and are in touch with the groups that affect them, and vice versa (each knows what the other is dealing with). That is the platform for the second aim, which is to change circumstances so that an organisation can achieve what it wants – whether selling its products, giving the best service in the world, or preventing the killing of whales. In doing so, the organisation will need to be responsive, adapting to the publics it is dealing with, changing its own shape and policies to make them acceptable. In short, organisations need to understand and reconcile the interests of groups that have a legitimate interest in their behaviour and prosperity, and to look out for those groups whose actions, disinterested or malevolent, could cause damage or create opportunities.

The Institute of Public Relations, recognising that its traditional definition is not one that is easily learned by those outside the business (nor by those inside), adopted in 1994 a phrase that is easily recalled and which will mean something to anyone: *Public relations is about reputation – the result of what you do, what you say and what others say about you.* It goes on to clarify public relations practice as: *the discipline which looks after reputation with the aim of earning understanding and support, and influencing opinion and behaviour.* In business this is undeniably a role of management and consequently fundamental to policy making (the most important area needing explanation or change in response to the attitudes of others).

Both simpler and more complex definitions exist. The simpler ones are usually popular travesties of the discipline. In a word: hype. Or tell only part of the story, as in the description given in the Economist's

MBA Pocket Guide: 'The art of presenting an organisation's views and interests in as favourable a light as possible to its many different constituencies: investors, customers, employees, legislators, environmentalists and so on.' Beware dictionaries too: 'The professional maintenance of a favourable public image, especially by a company or famous person.' And thesauruses: '. . . hype, ballyhoo, media coverage; public relations, PR, image-making, soft-sell, showmanship . . . '

The complex ones are not definitions but descriptions, listings of some of the procedures that make up public relations. The most quoted is the Mexican Statement of 1978: 'Public relations practice is the art and social science of analysing trends, predicting their consequences, counselling an organisation's leadership and implementing planned programmes of action which will serve both the organisation's and the public interest.'

1.3 Four steps to excellent PR

In the early 1980s Professor Jim Grunig of Maryland University began research into the public relations departments of large companies in America, Canada and, on a smaller scale, the United Kingdom. His aim was to propound and test a theory of excellence in public relations and communication management. He defined public relations as 'the management of communication between an organisation and its publics'. The study, made for the International Association of Business Communicators (IABC), divides into two parts: the theory of excellent PR itself and the results of the research into how PR is carried out and valued in some 300 companies, about 30 of them in the UK. The theory identifies four models of public relations.

Press agentry

Today this is represented by the efforts of organisations to obtain press, radio and TV coverage. What is news to the media is publicity for the company. The term had its origins in the press agents of the mid-nineteenth century. Grunig and his 1984 co-author Hunt sees them as the first full-time specialists to practise an aspect of public relations.

While public relations practitioners claim a wide spectrum for their work, time and again research shows that the most widespread activity is media relations, the press agentry of the 1990s. Press agentry, the excellence theory says, is one-way communication. The organisation puts out its statements – its messages – and hopes they will be covered.

By and large, when journalists use the material they inadvertently bolster the organisation's credibility (if only in that it is seen to be important enough to be reported and written about) and make people more aware of it. That, of course, is not their reason for writing the story.

Strictly, this is only one-way communication if the journalists follow the organisation's line. A knowledgeable journalist will put the information into the context of his experience, and it may be that his report will include facts and reactions that put the organisation in a different light. The moment the organisation's management becomes aware of this, a primitive form of two-way communication has taken place, with the potential for a change of policy (say) by the organisation, or at least greater understanding all round. Usually, however, a one-way message is intended, a picture is being painted, and this is close to propaganda.

Public information

The theory continues with another historical observation. Large corporations and government agencies in America suffered attacks from 'muckraking journalists' at the start of the twentieth century. The answer was for organisations to employ journalists themselves and they, knowing about the press, would prepare material for the press. They put out handouts which, says Grunig, 'generally were truthful and accurate' even if biased towards the organisation. The organisation is here not trying to manipulate its publics; it may be misrepresented in the media or have a complicated story to tell. It is simply putting out plain, unadorned information. This is the public information model of public relations. Again, it is essentially one-way; dialogue is minimal.

Government information services and official bodies generally see themselves as falling into this category. They are not trying to persuade, they would argue, but simply to inform. Others might see them as propagandists because they only put out selective information. Edward Bernays, in his 1920s book on propaganda, argued that the public didn't really think for itself. As it could only form its views through the information that filtered through to it via the mass media of the time, the thinking, he said, had already been done for it. When Bernays used the word 'propaganda', however, it had a softer sense than it has since acquired. It originally meant propagating a concept, a cause or a product.

Two-way asymmetrical public relations

Grunig has given his third model of public relations this mouthful of a name. It relates to Bernays' early work on harnessing behavioural and social sciences in the cause of public relations. (He is a nephew of Sigmund Freud and no stranger therefore to psychology.) Communication is two-way when an organisation uses research to understand people's motivations and find out what approaches and messages will make them think and act as the organisation wants. 'Practitioners both sought information from and gave information to publics,' says Grunig.

Communication is asymmetrical because it is unbalanced, unequal: the information sought isn't really for the good of the publics but rather to make the organisation more effective in maintaining its position. The organisation stays as it is, despite the research information, and tries to persuade the public to change. This seems less like manipulation than obduracy and obstinacy. Grunig's own comment was that organisations seem to believe that publics benefit from 'a lot of strange things . . . pollution, toxic waste, drinking, smoking, guns, overthrow of governments, dangerous products, lowered salary and benefits, discrimination against women and minorities, job lay-offs, dangerous manufacturing plants, risky transportation of products, political favoritism, insider trading, use of poisonous chemicals, exposure to carcinogens, nuclear weapons, and even warfare.'

Grunig's studies on the practicalities of how organisations in fact manage their public relations show that most companies are in asymmetrical mode. They use research and contact with their publics to help them understand how to motivate and persuade those publics.

Two-way symmetrical public relations

This brings us to the world as most people would privately like it to be, more mutually responsive. Symmetrical public relations is balanced; the organisation is willing to adjust to its publics even as it wants them to adjust to it. The research has genuine purpose: to aid communication, realignment, accommodation, concessions and understanding (in the sense of willingness to change).

Grunig sees the two-way symmetrical model of public relations as having the objective of understanding rather than persuading. He noted many of the attributes of two-way symmetrical public relations in the writings of early American practitioners. These 'included "telling the truth", "interpreting the client and public to one another" and "management understanding the viewpoints of employees and neighbors as well as employees and neighbors understanding the viewpoints of management".' However he did not believe that many practitioners put these ideas into practice. It was left, he argued, to 'public relations scholars and educators who took the practitioners at their word and made the model the basis of their teaching and research'. This is why he defines his theory as 'normative', not 'positive'; it explains how public relations *should* take place rather than what usually happens.

The central thesis of Grunig's book is, in fact, that public relations increases the effectiveness of an organisation by managing its interdependence with the publics that restrict its autonomy. The method is to build long-term stable relationships with its publics. The better the mutual understanding, he argues, the better the working relationship. This is his bid to convince management – what he calls the 'dominant coalition' of an organisation – that, fairly practised, public relations is not a threat to management's power but simply a better way for the organisation to achieve its aims.

The historical perspective to the theory helps understand it. The second half of the twentieth century has been characterised by burgeoning communications. Communications have brought everyone closer together, made the world smaller and smaller, more inter-dependent, less able to shy away from the problems of others. The growth of pressure groups has led to a greater acceptance on the part of large business corporations of the need to negotiate and compromise, to take notice of the needs of their most active and virulent publics. Particularly from the early 1980s, people came to realise that they ought not to treat the environment of the planet as though it were a raw material for the use of their generation alone. This, and greater emphasis on health and safety, has led to significant changes in the way organisations behave. They are increasingly likely under these circumstances to use two-way symmetrical public relations.

1.4 Related disciplines

It is important to be clear about the many other activities which are not synonymous with public relations but which come under its umbrella, and will often be part of a public relations programme.

Publicity

Publicity means sending out planned messages to further the interests of an organisation, product or person without specific payment to the media; the process by which something (a cause, idea, product, service, individual) becomes known, usually through the media. In local government, publicity is now defined as 'any communication, in whatever form, addressed to the public at large or to a section of the public'. Not included in this definition of publicity are 'defined groups of people' – specific publics as distinct from the general public. Though only a part of public relations, publicity is the most apparent; hence the close link between the two. Public relations will try to generate good publicity and counter or prevent bad publicity. Some people think 'any publicity is good publicity' (an idea which is supported by the MORI familiar-means-favourable 'rule'). Long after the unfavourable connotations of an incident have been forgotten the organisation may well remain familiar. But when the facts have gone from the mind – which mainly they do – an impression, a feeling is left which colours attitudes, opinions and behaviour. Organisations strive to obliterate the bad memories by replacing them with good ones. So, except when their objective is simply awareness, they certainly do not think that any publicity is good publicity.

Publicity is not necessarily something you seek. Public relations can be about keeping things out of the media, away from public knowledge. This need not be because there is something to hide: timing, confidentiality, judgement, advisability, understanding, resources, relevance, competitiveness and the public interest may all come into it.

Advertising

This is the easiest of all to define: bought space or time (specifically the traditional media bought through an advertising agency – press, radio, television, cinema, poster sites). The word is sometimes misused by business people because they think of it as the same as 'publicity' or 'free editorial'. If you pay for the space or time then (as long as your message is, in the words of the Advertising Standards Authority, 'legal, decent, honest') you can say what you wish. You control the message directly. Advertising can be used as part of a public relations programme, especially to persuade or to give information.

Sales promotion

Below-the-line expenditure which does not command agency commission (as do the five traditional forms of advertising). Editorial offers, in-store activities, vouchers and competitions are examples – literally, additional ways of promoting sales.

Communication

This is best written as communication rather than communications, to distinguish it from the telecommunications industry. In the 1990s there has been a move to 'communication management consultancy' with the idea of creating a clearly delineated service for internal and external information exchange. This was triggered by the substantial culture shifts companies have been experiencing in managing changes in organisational structure and markets. Internal communication, often previously paid only lip-service by hierarchical managements, suddenly became a priority. Communication is passing on information and ideas to others and, in the public relations arena at least, listening and acting on the responses. Public relations people regard communication more as the technical side of what they do, the tactical results of planning, the way messages that have been decided strategically are passed on (by newsletter, E-mail, team briefing, video, press article and so on).

The idea of total communication means co-ordinating every aspect of internal and external communication. The need for this may be obvious but in a company of any size, or which employs enthusiastic people in different departments, conflicting messages may emerge in very different styles. For example, one might order golf umbrellas, remembering the company logo but forgetting the slogan; another might have prepared letters in response to reader enquiries from advertising coverage without realising that new literature was ready. The problem seems no easier to solve in small companies than large ones where human resources, public affairs, advertising and marketing departments all need to relate to each other. It may be even harder as more companies become 'virtual', having no central offices because staff can work from networked computers.

Sponsorship

What people think of an organisation is partly conditioned by who or what it associates with. Sponsorship, therefore, becomes an active way of reaching into people's minds. The Carling Premiership. British Fuels and the rugby football league. Holsten and Spurs. Smith Klein Beecham: Lynford Christie and Lucozade. Imperial Tobacco's Embassy Challenge fishing competition. BT and the play, Shakespeare's Country. Esso and The Million Tree Campaign. Arthur Andersen and the ABSA (Association for Business Sponsorship of the Arts) awards. The sponsor contributes to or pays for the cost of an event or events, or for a team or competitor, in sport or the arts, in return for marketing and promotion rights.

Association of ideas is a powerful phenomenon and, even more to the point, television is a wide-ranging medium. Sponsorships are not altruistic, nor should they be on the chairman's whim. The return on investment is usually the increasing awareness of a name; or the link with something wholesome and caring, or of importance to a community; a boost for product sales; improved staff relations.

Sponsorship provides opportunities for corporate hospitality and ways of appealing to specific audiences, especially those who enjoy sports or the arts, or who are concerned with charities.

Media relations

Before television attained its present dominance and before radio stations proliferated, media relations was known as press relations. This led to a confusion with public relations, and what business people meant when they said: 'We need some PR.' They are still likely to say this when they read about their competitors in the papers, hear them on a phone-in or watch them on TV. The press – or media – release is still the most commonly known, ill-prepared (in the eyes of journalists) and over-used, tool of media relations.

Media relations plays a huge part in public relations work, often being the greater part of activity. The media, because they are the conduits through which information, opinions and ideas flow out to the public at large, have an immense power over how people think and behave. In the world of business, company directors can become dismayed if a competitor dominates the news, or the trade press of their business. 'Where's our share?' they are apt to ask. Journalists, 'gatekeepers' because of their selectivity, are also a public in themselves; they may not use material sent to them but it still may influence their views.

The stock-in-trade of media relations is:

- careful preparation of information to be used in news releases or media packs (a folder of relevant facts and background)

- telephone conversations to give – and discover – information
- press conferences (or news or media conferences, it doesn't matter) when a story is important enough to announce personally to all interested journalists
- meetings with one journalist for background or a special story
- meetings with a small group of journalists, usually from media which do not compete with each other
- invitations to hospitality events for familiarity and to build a relationship
- facility visits
- photo calls and stunts (trying to make a mundane subject interesting).

None of these activities is synonymous with public relations but all are part of it from time to time. They represent different forms of contact with the publics that matter to an organisation, and greater or lesser degrees of dialogue and feedback.

Marketing

In some organisations marketing directors have control over public relations. Where the PR supports marketing this is logical. But public relations also has a scale and scope beyond marketing: it helps create and modify the context within which marketing works. The Chartered Institute of Marketing defines marketing as: 'The management process responsible for identifying, anticipating and satisfying consumer requirements profitably'. In short, producing what people want and selling it to them at a profit.

The prevalent management idea that everyone remotely connected with an organisation is a 'customer' rather obscures the difference between 'publics' and 'markets'. Added to that, 1990s marketers have propagated the idea of 'marketing relationships'; this takes satisfying the customer (at a profit) deep into the territory of public relations. Even so, there are two obvious distinctions. Marketing selects targets; publics affect you whether you select them or not. Marketing is about sales of products or services; public relations is also about the conditions that make those sales possible.

Another group of terms describes particular types of public relations practice. These are concerned with finance, investment and lobbying; the management of issues and crises; and internal and external relations.

Financial public relations

This involves establishing relations and information flow with the City and financial community, including the financial media, analysts who study specific business sectors, and shareholders. You should be careful to differentiate between financial public relations for ordinary public companies that are listed on the Stock Exchange, and for the financial institutions (such as building societies and insurance companies) which have financial products to sell. They are offering financial services with money simply as the product.

Companies have to report their figures at set times, produce annual accounts and hold an annual general meeting. All will be examined by analysts who study and pronounce upon profit performances in different industrial sectors, by financial journalists who make their own judgements for their newspapers and magazines, by competitors, and by prospective shareholders (numerate private people as well as insurance companies, unit trusts and investment houses who are the powerful institutional investors companies need to build relationships with).

Investor relations (IR)

This is a new discipline which has grown up within the loose framework of financial public relations. Large companies whose securities are publicly traded now have IR departments to manage relationships with existing or potential shareholders.

Their function is to ensure that a company's shares are fairly valued, in the short and long term, and that everyone has the same honest and accurate information at the same time. Other aims for this IR function might be to preserve access to the capital markets on the most favourable terms, to maintain liquidity for the company's securities and to ensure a two-way flow of information which benefits both investors and management.

Lobbying and public affairs

Another sector of public relations which has a mystique all of its own is that known as government affairs or, more generally, public affairs. As in financial PR, practitioners work in a world with its own rules and special knowledge. The importance of government and public affairs has increased as the EU has become a greater influence on parliament, and as the world has become more interconnected. Lobbying is the specific effort to influence public decision-making either by seeking a change in the law or trying to prevent a change. As such it will be issue-related.

Government relations (or affairs) has wider connotations and is concerned long term with developing relationships with government and bodies which decide public policies and legislation. Councillors, MPs, civil servants, Euro MPs and the bureaucracy of Brussels are all publics for government affairs practitioners. From January 1995, PR people lobbying professionally were required to register their interests with their membership bodies, for public examination.

Issues management

Spotting danger a long way off is part of modern public relations strategy. Then approaches to external changes can be included in policy. By monitoring what is happening in the world – the incipient issues which affect organisations – steps can be taken to lessen or nullify their impact or to adapt the organisation early to the inevitable.

This is the often emphasised function of PR being the eyes and ears of an organisation. Issues range from changes in rules or laws to trends like environmental protection or market shifts.

Crisis management

This is a public relations discipline to help organisations anticipate the bad things that can happen to them and be prepared. Accidents, strikes, explosions: systems should be ready to deal with them, teams chosen and rehearsed, communication procedures known and practised.

Internal communication

The organisation's relationship and communications with its employees and with the networks of people who work with the company.

External relations

Some companies think of their relationships as divided into two: those within the organisation and those outside it. If internal relations is to do with staff and departments, external relations is everything else. The term is often used when the personnel department (human resources) handles all internal communication and the company wants to stress the management of external relationships, particularly public affairs.

Information officers

Government and many public bodies adopt this title to avoid any undertones of persuasion. The consequence is that dialogue – which is two-way communication – becomes limited.

Propaganda

Finally, it is essential to distinguish between public relations and propaganda. This is especially difficult given that the ultimate aim of organisations is usually to control an agenda of issues and to get people to do what the organisations want.

It is also a pity that the word propaganda – which means simply to propagate, grow, spread an idea – has acquired bad connotations. In war and conflict you expect propaganda because morale must be kept up and only one point of view can be allowed – or the war may be lost. It is naive, too, to think that organisations in peace time do not tell lies to get what they want. But that isn't public relations, and it jeopardises credibility.

There are three qualities that mark professional public relations out from propaganda. Professor Tim Traverse-Healy, a long-time practitioner turned academic, isolated them in a paper on propaganda for the International Public Relations Association. First, the existence of a code of conduct which forbids lying (though not the withholding of the truth). Secondly, care for what is in the public interest. Thirdly, preparedness for dialogue, compromise, negotiation, response; a willingness to change stance, attitude and behaviour. Propaganda is wholly one-sided and closed; public relations is about dialogue, and open.

2

——— PRACTICE: ———
THE PR PROCESS

2.1 Simple structures for campaign planning

PR academic and practitioner Dr Jon White insists that 'there is a clear process' to public relations work. The oldest guide of all is also the shortest: the mnemonic RACE.

- **Research**, analyse, define problems
- **Action** programme and budget
- **Communicate**, carry out the programme
- **Evaluation**: monitor, modify.

This sequence of thought is only common sense; you can't write a PR proposal any other way. You have to find out the facts, draw up a plan, carry out the plan, and decide how effective it has been so that you can improve your communications, or change your strategy.

Frank Jefkins' six-point plan expands this:

- Appreciate the situation – communication audit
- Define the objectives
- Decide the publics
- Select the media, channels, techniques
- Set the budget
- Assess the results.

An easy way to remember in more detail the elements needed in your public relations programme is to memorise this sentence as a mnemonic:

Question and analyse; set objectives; decide publics, messages, strategy and plan; cost; communicate; and assess the results.

- **Question and analyse**

  You can't start unless you ask questions (a simpler term than 'research', which conjures up the heavy guns of MORI and Gallup). Unless you ask questions you can't start thinking. You will find you are still asking questions when you are well past that first stage, because you are continuing to think.

  A popular framework for asking questions is to use a SWOT analysis. This is the simplest way of analysing an organisation's position in any given situation. It is regularly used in marketing appreciations and usually makes it clear where public relations work is needed. Look for:

  Strengths   What is the organisation good at? Where is it better than its competitors? How strong is its reputation?

  Weaknesses   Where is the organisation vulnerable? What can be done to strengthen it? Can channels of communication be improved?

  Opportunities   What is happening in the market place? What's new? Where is the competition weak?

  Threats   Are changes taking place that might weaken the organisation? What is the legal position? Are competitors about to become more aggressive? What is changing? Are internal communications sound?

FOR MOST COMPLEX CAMPAIGNS THERE ARE TEN QUESTIONS TO ASK

1 What information?
2 To which publics?
3 What are their characteristics?
4 What issues interest them? What are their needs?
5 What channels of communication for each?
6 What are the characteristics and biases of those channels?
7 Where is the information to come from? Check its accuracy.
8 What is our strategy for designing the specific messages to meet our objectives? What methods of persuasion can we use?
9 What is the key message? What are its main points?
10 How can non-verbal cues such as colour, sound, music, packaging, be used in support?

Nager and Allen

Having asked the questions you will have some answers. This will help you think more purposefully: analysing the answers will define the scope of your enquiry and you can then think in more depth, more specifically.

- **Set objectives**

  From the research you will be able to assess the position and work out what your objectives should be. PR people are encouraged to see that specific objectives are set, partly because it is easier to think about something that is quantifiable rather than general, and partly because what is quantifiable is by definition measurable, which means in turn that it can be evaluated.

  Evaluation takes place at the end of the process – sometimes during it as well – but it needs to be thought about and decided when the objectives are set. As there are often beneficial spin-offs during a campaign it is foolish to judge an otherwise constructive programme as a failure because it did not fully achieve its aims. It might, for instance, convince a client or manager of the virtuosity of public relations, of the need for a PR element in everything the organisation does; it might stimulate unforeseen but good results. Some excellent campaigns fail, especially in the political sector. This does not make them bad campaigns (you can play well and still lose). Some activities are doomed before they start (like many Ten Minute Motions in the House of Commons) but they increase awareness, imply a volition, a bandwagon. Canny PR people build that into their proposals. But don't allow your organisation to set unobtainable or vague objectives; you will find your thinking simply seizes up.

  As with evaluation, you will be thinking about the costs of everything as you work your way through the process. It will certainly not help anyone's cause if the aims are far beyond the budget. In fact, you will find yourself revising aims, publics, evaluation and budget, as well as the programme itself, throughout your drafting.

- **Decide publics**

  Plan the activities for a campaign by thinking carefully about the individual groups affected. What are their self-interests? What is their nature? What is the message for them?

- **Strategy, and plan and messages**

  Standard wisdom is that you work out your strategy (how to achieve your objectives) and then use tactics (PR techniques) accordingly. Your strategy is your decision to get from A to B; your plan is the detail of how you get there. Within that plan will be certain tactical options. You may well change your tactics while maintaining your strategy. Impending failure may bring about a change in strategy.

● **Cost**

You need to have a rough idea of budget to begin with because this will influence what you propose. You then need to cost every part of the programme to check that it is affordable.

● **Communication programme**

This is the plan of campaign, the activities you think up to reach the different publics, the communicating part of public relations. Material and events will overlap but if you don't keep separate publics in mind you will not respond to their differing needs.

Techniques used in PR are everything that will aid communication between people and groups. They include: letters (and their tone); newsletters (and how interesting they are); videos; leaflets;

The alphabet comes in handy for remembering things. In marketing it's the four Ps: product, price, place, promotion. In public relations, try the eight Cs:

Credibility   the recipient of a message must have confidence, trust, belief in its sender
Context   communication should be appropriate to the environment in which it is made
Content   the message must have meaning for the recipient and fit in with their social and cultural values
Clarity   the message must be in simple terms so that it can be understood
Continuity   communication is a continuing process in which repetition is helpful to the memory and understanding
Consistency   is needed for credibility
Channels   use channels of communication familiar to, and respected by, the recipient
Capability   the nature of the recipient, their habits, culture, ability, must be taken into account.

---

posters; signs; media coverage; research (which in itself is a form of communication – saying we care what you think – and whose findings can later be used as the basis for further communication); events; sponsorship; meetings; any and every way of making contact, influencing attitudes, changing behaviour, achieving mutual understanding, reinforcing reputation.

- **Assess the results**

  People working in public relations are keen for their occupation to become more scientific. But including evaluation as an element can inhibit the setting of objectives (there is no point in being too ambitious and 'failing' when you can be less ambitious and 'succeed'). Probably the more useful forms of evaluation are those that take place during a programme and which can be used to change direction, modify activities, re-emphasise a message which is not getting across or which is being misinterpreted.

The proposal

You tailor this to the nature of the campaign. A simple and coherent structure to adopt is that advised in the distance learning course for the CAM Diploma in public relations:

- **Introduction** The project, context, current position
- **Background** Summary of useful information; research
- **Objectives** Which should be achievable
- **Strategy** The messages
- **Tactics** The activities, publics, timetable
- **Resources** Budget, people's time, assistance
- **Evaluation** Touchstones for success.

A more complex planning matrix is from 'Strategic programme planning' by B. E. Hainsworth (1992), published in the *American Public Relations Review*, Vol. **18**, No 1. It is used by students on the Stirling University post-graduate course:

- **Research**

  1 *Background* Synthesis of primary and secondary research, history, current trends in opinion and attitudes

  2 *Situation analysis* Short statement of the current situation and problem

3   *Central difficulty*   One-sentence encapsulation of the problem and harm if it is not resolved

4   *Start to identify publics and resources*   The individuals and organisations affected by the situation or who can intervene in its resolution.

● **Planning**

5   *Campaign goals*   What you want to achieve to resolve the central problem

6   *Objectives*   Specific, measurable, attainable results within a given time-scale which will help achieve the goals

7   *Key publics*   Those audiences (constituencies) you must reach to be successful with the campaign.

8   *Specific strategies*   For each public so that you reach them with the messages

9   *Tactics*   What tactics or media tools will support each strategy? You will need several, each a conduit of the message for the strategy.

● **Communication**

10   *The messages*   The final versions, refined for each public and including that public's self-interest (giving them a reason to support you)

11   *Summary*   Construct a simple table to ensure you have covered everything, that your plan can meet the campaign objectives

12   *Calendar*   Chart the steps, with approximate timings

13   *Budget*   The cost of each action.

● **Evaluation**

14   *Evaluation criteria*   How you will judge if each objective and goal has been attained

15   *Evaluation tools*   The timing and cost of each (include in points 12 and 13).

As with any report or proposal, how far you go into possibilities depends on the size of the challenge. Don't waste time with a mighty sledge-hammer of a plan to crack a nut-like problem. Very often light research, a logical plan and creative communications will suffice. Sometimes you need to do a lot of research and thinking to come up with a very simple plan that looks as though it has been thought up overnight. Occasionally you need to go the whole hog, work through it all very carefully and put it down on paper step by step.

Be clear that many entrepreneurs have rudimentary plans like this in their minds without working their way methodically through everything. The thought processes are automatic. By the time your plan has emerged such people may have done most of it and be on to something else. That's why they are entrepreneurs.

2.2 From public to publics

Public relations began, as a term, with the idea of communicating with the general public and worrying about, or influencing, what they thought. Relations with the public as a whole are an impossibility for organisations, even with mass communication techniques, and an irrelevance. 'Public' gradually narrowed its meaning. The Institute of Public Relations used to end its definition of the discipline: '. . . between an organisation and its public.' Here 'public' had the meaning: those people who matter to an organisation and affect it. They, naturally, are not homogeneous; they fall roughly into different groups, each with a common interest, characteristic or boundary. So in 1987 the IPR changed 'public' to 'publics'.

The starting point to thinking about public relations, therefore, is to consider who the publics are that concern you. They depend on the type of organisation you work for or the project you are concerned with. Consider the publics of the following organisations.

Local government

Elected councillors
Staff
Trade unions
Electors
Residents
Council tax payers
Users of services
Other local authorities in the area
Local authority associations
Residents' associations
Community associations
Local business and commerce
Visitors to the area
Potential visitors to the area
Potential investors
Potential residents
Government departments
Members of Parliament – Commons and Lords
Members of the European Parliament

This list is taken from *Public relations for local government*. The authors point out that the list would have to be revised and added to depending on the tier of local government – for example, councils may have to consider pupils and parents, road users, the elderly, tenants of council homes or users of leisure facilities.

By making positive decisions about specific groups or individual publics, you are then able to make more informed decisions about which means of communication to select for each category. The approach to a potential investor in the area would be very different from that chosen for the local Member of Parliament or a resident or a member of staff.

City and financial

The financial publics relevant to a company which has its shares quoted on the stock exchange are different again:

Self-investing institutions	Stockbroking firms
Pension funds	Equity salesmen
Insurance companies	Research analysts
Investment trusts	Merchant bank corporate
Unit trusts	finance
Fund management groups	Employee shareholders
Merchant bank fund	Private investors
managers	
Investment management	
companies	

These are publics specific to investor relations. But many other groups are interested in a company's financial performance:

Customers	Trade unions
Suppliers	Banks
Government	Competitors
Local authorities	Overseas publics
Parliament	Professional intermediaries:
Statutory bodies	accountants, solicitors,
Employees	bank managers, stockbrokers

These lists may appear daunting but they demonstrate the need to think long and hard however simple it may seem at first to identify your publics. To think about them coherently, categorise them in terms of importance and judge them in terms of menace. Philip Lesly, in his *Handbook of Public Relations and Communication*, lists the groups that are likely to be important over most issues: employees and their families, government and regulatory bodies, third-party experts and academics, mutual aid coalitions, the local community, unofficial opinion leaders, stockholders, the financial community, customers. Significantly, he adds to these: potential allies, potential critics, probable neutrals; and dissidents, activists, advocates, zealots and fanatics. You will not wish to upset your allies nor give weapons to your enemies, so you will approach them differently.

Issues management

It is in issues management that the importance of thinking deeply in terms of the nature of different publics makes itself most felt. When people or groups come together in reaction to a common problem, they become an identifiable public. (They may have got together over an unsatisfactory product, a poor service, factory pollution or something that is not happening which they think should.) The degree to which they feel they can do something about that problem defines whether they are likely to be active or passive publics, how far they are likely to communicate their feelings. Parallel to this is how important they feel the problem is, how far they will go to do something about it. In short, how far they feel involved. The more involved people become the more they will seek information (and not necessarily from the organisations they query or oppose). This is how new publics come into existence. The environmental causes of the 1980s and 90s are typical examples.

A theory of publics

Using this style of thinking you can see how a theory of publics can be developed to help organisations see potential danger. You can group people in four ways. The Wimps are both disinterested in the organisation and do not think they can alter its behaviour. The Frustrates are concerned about the problem and would, ideally, like to do something about it but in practice feel nothing they do will change things. Close to these are the Fatalists who relate to the problem but think it is a waste of time to try to change it. On the other hand Activists definitely think they can change the organisation's behaviour and that it's worth trying.

Professor Jim Grunig published such a study in 1982. He had longer names for the publics he identified but those, broadly, were the groupings. He followed this up with another study of how different people reacted to a range of related issues. This produced a parallel classification. All-issue publics were active on all the problems. Apathetic publics ignored all the problems (clearly activists and wimps). He then divided the remaining activists into two groups. One group works on a single issue that concerns only a few people (say on whales). The other works on a single issue that affects nearly everyone (say drinking and driving). These he calls single-issue publics and hot-issue publics respectively. Such research and publics-related thinking he calls 'situational theory'. It is invaluable as a background idea in planning PR programmes in relation to publics (although the theory seems to have been applied more by academics and students in their research than by business people).

Other ways of segmenting publics abound. One method chooses priority audiences and divides them into primary, intervening and special publics; that is, those directly affected, those through whom you could communicate (say parents or children), and any organised groups. Another way of thinking about them is latent publics, aware publics and active publics: people who are unaware there is a problem, people who realise there is a problem but are not organised, and those who are organised.

In consumer PR, where you are seeking acceptance of a new product, some people seize on innovations immediately (innovators), others take it up soon after (early adopters) and some are not enthusiastic for quite a while (followers). Where you could identify them, they would be different publics requiring different messages to persuade them at different times. This process is known in the academic world as the diffusion of innovation. Publics emerge from the environment in which an organisation operates. The most obvious relate to the organisation's immediate functions: suppliers, employees, customers, advisers. The next layer is that of the controlling groups that enable the organisation to function: regulatory bodies and shareholders for example. Normative publics are the groups that share common interests, like trade associations. Finally, the activists again: the pressure groups or any informal grouping that may affect the company.

One dogged individual, especially over a *cause célèbre*, can cause a company all kinds of grief, and is thus a discrete public. Geography can be country, county or locality. Demography is age, job, education, sex, income. Both groupings can produce definable publics. Lifestyle has emerged in the last quarter of the century to subdefine direct mail targets. As these are grouped on the principle that birds of a feather flock together, they can have as powerful connotations for public relations thinking as for marketing. The Prizm system has 40 categories for Americans, all with colourful and succinct nicknames like Grey Power (older upper middle-class communities) or Money and Brains (clusters of white-collar intellectuals). Opinion formers exist in every type of community: MPs, journalists, solicitors, people of position, reputation, standing and influence.

Given that a public is, in the definition of sociologist John Dewey, a community that develops around a shared problem or concern, the coming of electronic on-line link-up systems, like the Internet or the Delphi Forum, has created what are becoming known as virtual publics. These, says Dr John Pavlik of Columbia University, New York, completely 'redefine the mobilisation timeframe' for publics. 'In a matter of minutes, even seconds, a world-wide public, potentially numbering millions, can mobilise electronically around a problem perceived initially by even just a single computer user.'

2.3 Market research

Research is the starting point for public relations. You need to know what the facts are, what has gone before, what the background is, what people think, what the competition is doing. In a small way, research of a kind has always helped PR consultancies in their pitches for new business. A straw poll of the media and other reachable publics used to work wonders in producing a view of the prospective client. Research is also an important factor in public relations being seen by business people as a professional discipline.

Desk research

Research need not be formal. At its simplest it is desk research. You look up information in the library, collect newspaper cuttings on an issue, make calls to trade and professional bodies. Follow your nose – but make sure you narrow down the research or you will spend endless, tedious hours writing off for company brochures, reading journals, tracking down special reports in the nationals, traipsing round exhibitions, contacting market research companies for existing studies, sifting through government sources (like the Census, official statistics, *Business Monitor*). Never overlook the help that editorial departments of trade journals may be willing to give, at least in guiding you to sources for their sector.

Electronic databases abound. You can tap into these through your computer and modem. Some store statistics, others have complete issues of publications. The danger here is collecting too much chaotic information, so once again you have to narrow down the search. The secret of effective database searching is defining keywords.

Desk research is also an essential precursor to planning campaigns in Europe, at least to identify some benchmark statistics country by country before the real thinking begins. Typical starting points might be the Department of Trade, embassies, the Central Office of Information, chambers of commerce or directories like *Reader's Digest Eurodata*. Always ask whoever you consult what other sources they can suggest.

Primary research

Desk research is secondary research: it exists already. Primary research is when you set up the mechanics of finding things out by conducting your own research survey. This is of two kinds, quantitative and qualitative.

Within quantitative research you survey a representative sample of the public you are interested in. You want statistics and measurements on which to base your campaign. This tends to be used to yield good material for the media, underpin campaigns and measure effectiveness. With a quota (or stratified) sample the interviewers have to find certain categories of people (old, bald, butter-eating, 23–28 years of age) in proportion to their numbers in the population as a whole. With random samples people are selected literally at random, say from a list, or street by street. There has to be a watertight random method to make sure there is no hidden bias to distort the sample.

With qualitative research you are looking for views, opinions and insights and these are usually obtained through lengthy interviews or in discussion groups of six or eight carefully selected people. You can use it to clarify problems by identifying attitudes. If you are lucky, just one person can open eyes to a solution.

Many research projects use both quantitative and qualitative methods. For example, Shell Expro, whose business is in oil exploration, organise a Lifestyle programme to help employees with their mental, social and physical well-being. They thought their employees were apathetic about it and so commissioned both types of research. They had discussions with small groups of employees (also known as focus groups) to stimulate new ideas. Armed with this information they sent their 8000 onshore and off-shore employees a questionnaire and developed a new Lifestyle programme from the answers.

CASE STUDY

Cold sore cream

You can see how research can be closely integrated with a public relations campaign from this Wellcome Foundation study:

Objectives To increase cold sore consultations with doctors by 200,000 in a year, as a means of increasing sales of Zovirax cream and tablets.

Target publics The general public (eight million people in the UK suffer from cold sores) and health professionals (GPs, dentists, practice nurses, health visitors, midwives, opticians and occupational health staff).

Research A survey was made of 1000 adults over 18, representative of the population as a whole, at more than 65 sampling points chosen by a random location method, and interviewed at home. This research was used to decide the strategy for the campaign by finding out why people did not consult their doctor or dentist and what would persuade the public to go for treatment. Forty-three per cent said they would see their doctor if they knew there was an effective treatment. Distant, vague promises will not overcome consumer apathy. Sufferers also needed to realise, the research showed, that cold sores can be serious and contagious.

So the findings established the messages for the campaign: there is a cure; cold sores are unsightly, hurt and put other people off; and they are contagious (67 per cent did not know that). Finally the research produced regional statistics (for the local press) and quirky angles for TV, radio, women's and health professional press. Cold sores became 'The big turn-off at parties'; kissing and St Valentine's day were two ready-made vehicles for press releases.

Media programme The PR campaign included live and down-the-line radio interviews with doctors chosen because they came over well, TV interviews in the health spots of magazine programmes and articles in health professional journals. The campaign also included mass distribution of a cold sore health education pack with poster and leaflets to waiting rooms and clinics, and endorsements from professional bodies.

This was an example of using research to develop activities within a public relations programme. Other uses of research are when it becomes the activity itself, as a media hook, and when it is used to measure how effective a campaign is. For journalists, research surveys are good copy, giving them an instant story through statistics and forecasts; but make sure the statistics are valid.

Financial sector research

Research can be applied to any PR sector. Some, however, need more intrinsic understanding from the research company than others. An instance is the world of investor relations (IR), where the aim is to keep investors happy, informed and investing in the company. Research can find out about investor and financial commentator attitudes to the company, how they make their decisions and what they know about a company. A problem IR practitioners have met is in the interpretation of the survey results and this may best be tackled jointly by researcher and IR professionals.

Surveys might be conducted among institutional investors – shareholders and potential shareholders – analysts, financial media and private shareholders (a much smaller and less powerful group than the big institutions like banks and unit trusts). One 1990 survey found that institutional investors most often turned to analysts and the analysts to the company. The financial journalists contact both the company and the analysts, and what they write is read by fund managers and analysts. The survey found that, for analysts, after direct contact with the company, the annual report was the most important source of information.

Research into how a particular company was rated showed relative ignorance among fund managers about its strategy and the quality of its management. This brought about a change in the investor relations programme so that institutional fund managers were mailed direct, and a programme of news releases, one-to-one meetings and small group presentations was introduced. When the annual results were announced the company made a presentation to analysts.

Some PR applications

Contact some of the leading research companies when you want to know if research already exists on a subject or want ideas on what you might do. You can have a question included quite cheaply in regular 'omnibus' surveys by the big market research companies (like Gallup).

CASE STUDY

The sleep survey

Dunlopillo make latex beds and pillows. Over 15 months they conducted research into sleep habits and patterns to help product development and support Dunlopillo's marketing strategy (to be the key authority on sleep).

The research findings showed that Scots enjoy a better night's sleep than people living in England, that people who snore have the most car accidents, that 12 million people wheeze every night, and that 'nightcaps' are drunk more in England than in Scotland.

The PR consultants, Infopress, turned the research findings into a 'story'. They combined the ideas of having an authoritative speaker, interesting research findings and a 'popular' approach to getting them across to achieve national and local coverage. Early morning interviews were arranged, with Dunlopillo's managing director appearing on Sky TV and Dr Colin Shapiro of Edinburgh University, who conducted the research, on the Today radio programme. A photocall was held at the Savoy Hotel. Dr Shapiro – by now dubbed 'Dr Sleep' – lay in bed in a nightshirt in the Savoy's riverside gardens. He was photographed being served breakfast in bed by a Page 3 model.

The press conference was at 11 am and included home editors and medical correspondents. After the press conference Dr Sleep and Dunlopillo's MD, on separate telephone lines, gave over 20 radio interviews at five-minute intervals. At the press lunch which followed journalists were able to ask more questions.

The following morning's press had headlines like 'Wakey, wakey' and 'Crashing snores', and the research proved excellent material for the cartoonists.

Mintel have observed that the press themselves use research as back-up to news stories or to create them. A network of 400 field-workers in some 130 countries report back on consumer product prices. To attract attention to the service Mintel conducted their own 'World in a Shopping Basket' survey, looking at the prices of 22 everyday products across 13 countries. This triggered plenty of coverage of the 'Bargain basement for beans not booze' variety and plenty of highly edible bar charts and diagrams (an illustration helps a story). Mintel does similar checks on the prices of services, leisure and clothing.

Bob Worcester of MORI says that the main technological advance will be in neural networking: the ability to cross reference using computers. It analyses data to determine, he says, 'inter-relationships and curious correlations'. He thinks MORI's Buy Test, a way of pre-testing advertisement effectiveness, could be used to test announcements to employees, or how well the chairman's statement in the report and accounts will be received. MORI also, through its new subsidiary Socioconsult, studies consumer and social trends in Europe and North America for the effects they will have on business. At conferences, one of the most audience-attracting sessions you can set up is a futures forecast from a research company like Henley Centre.

MORI investigates opinion-formers' knowledge of and attitudes to companies, organisations and industry sectors (although they are best known for political opinion polling it is only four per cent of their business). They examine various sections of government, the financial community, business leaders, the media, the general public (corporate tracking, business and the environment, and corporate social responsibility) and student attitudes.

For quick checks on attitudes about specific issues you can use telephone surveys. These are mainly conducted now using CATI (Computer Assisted Telephone Interviewing). This approach can be used to find out what customers think about your product, your service, your after-sales service, and how they match up to your competitors'. The other popular system is CAPI (computerised personal interviewing).

Consumer tracking studies – regularly following the progress of products so that action can be taken quickly when things go wrong – are conducted by companies like Neilsen using their huge electronic databases and panels of several thousand householders. Studies can be broken down into product types (durables, electricals, do-it-yourself and so on). One system monitors prescriptions. Another collects barcode readings. Yet another meters what people watch on television.

Press releases about the results of a survey need scrutinising for conclusions that may not be part of the findings, that are simply the views of whoever wrote the release, never mind the researcher. You should always look at the questions that were asked and, if you are conducting a survey, send them out with the report. Research reports are a popular way for clients and management to get what they want – well, it's true, the research shows. But are the questions objective or are they leading questions? Are they in any way ambiguous? Are the conclusions sound? If repeated, ought the research to produce similar results? That forty-six per cent of people are against something may be given as a strong reason for your being against it too. Never forget that fifty-four per cent are not against it; they may be equivocal or for. A percentage difference like that is enough to vote a country into the Common Market. The worst example, as happened on a television audience discussion programme, is when 49 per cent for and 51 per cent against something is translated as 'most people are against'. True, but . . .

2.4 Communication audits

Historically, PR has lacked clout in the boardroom. It has been regarded as the messenger: blamed and killed when the message is read. With authoritarian boards, sealed off from the battlefields, disinterested in change, PR tended to do as it was bid: handle the press, obtain favourable publicity. If PR did take part in strategy and planning this tended to be in the narrow sector of communication which management, at its worst, thought of as free advertising. Framing policy came before communication, and was no part of public relations.

With the breakdown of traditional trading and working environments, greater government say in business conditions, the high-tech revolution and new methods of communication (from tele-conferencing to interactive video), public relations has been presented with new opportunities where it can take the lead in 'being the eyes and ears of the organisation'. The power of pressure groups and new business considerations like the environment, have allowed PR to get a hand on the steering wheel from time to time.

What had been missing also for PR was a recognisable process, a logical, repeatable series of steps, a method. Flair and insight are invaluable but not practicable. The management mind (though not necessarily the entrepreneurial) needs to see a discipline at work. That was what was behind the introduction of public relations as an option on the Cranfield MBA course when it started in 1986. It lapsed after a few years – showing only that the idea had still not penetrated enough boardrooms – then started up again at City University, London, in 1994.

Crisis management demonstrated that sound PR principles could be applied systematically to aid corporate survival. The technical procedures of flotations and takeovers did likewise, with PR professionals gaining growing respect (and fees) from the principals and the merchant banks. The value of sound and honest communication in the City – beyond giving stories to the financial press and helping with financial reporting – became recognised. Companies now planned their relationships with institutional investors and analysts.

The existence of PR systems that could be bought and used in a similar way to accounting or legal services – they had recognisable, repeatable structures – helped the idea of the communication audit, a clearly defined and recognised 'methodology' for planning corporate identity, into the boardroom. Who are we? At least, who do we think we are? How are we regarded by our publics (or 'constituencies'). The difference between what an organisation believes it is and stands for, and how other people regard its activities, is often called the communication gap. As PR people are fond of saying these days, it's all about perceptions. The communication audit is about comparing those perceptions with the organisation's own view of itself.

A strong sense of corporate identity is the driving force for everyone in a company, the essence of how it differentiates itself from its competitors, the backbone of the reputation that sees policies through with government, City and customers. MORI research has demonstrated that the acceptance of products by the consumer depends greatly on corporate reputation – what people think of the company. The company becomes the brand: it needs to be packaged, differentiated from similar products, positioned in the market place (which for a business includes relations with local and central government, the City, the local community and suppliers). In short, corporate identity is now constructed by an infinitely more complex process than the corporate advertising and designer-led approaches that used to hold sway (say in the 1970s). It creates the strategy, plans and tactics which enable the board to manage its corporate environment so that people outside the company realise what the company is about.

Reginald Watts, deputy chairman of Citigate Corporate, uses the auditing process shown in Fig. 2.1. The objective of the corporate positioning is to be effective and believable, and 'genuinely to reflect the life, culture and values of a company'. It is then more likely to be memorable. He sees the communication audit as an intrinsic part of what he calls

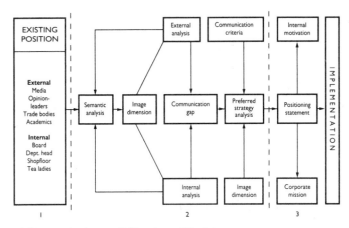

Fig. 2.1 Communication audit (Courtesy: Citigate)

'perception management', and the lynch pin for the new idea that businesses can manage their trading environments. 'It has grown,' he says, 'out of a combination of traditional corporate public relations and corporate identity.' In summary the process is:

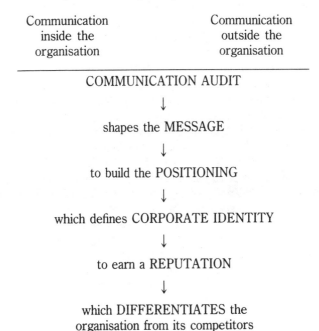

Communication
inside the
organisation

Communication
outside the
organisation

COMMUNICATION AUDIT

↓

shapes the MESSAGE

↓

to build the POSITIONING

↓

which defines CORPORATE IDENTITY

↓

to earn a REPUTATION

↓

which DIFFERENTIATES the
organisation from its competitors

The communication audit begins by finding out what people inside and outside the company think of it. Out of the interviews will come a bundle of impressions, some sharp, some erroneous (but fact in some people's minds nevertheless). The audit persuades the directors to take notice of (what to them are) erroneous perceptions, and to make it a springboard for action. It should also warn that internally perhaps all is not consistent. The responses will vary, conflict, miss or match the directors' own views of the company. Comparing the differences between what outsiders and insiders think leads to clarifying the company's present image and assessing the communication gap.

A central positioning statement is drawn up – one good solid message, chosen from several possible similar messages that sum up the company. It must convey the three or four main characteristics of the company that have emerged and also be capable of being communicated through the various channels available. It is now used as a central reference point for all external communication. (It's called singing from the same song sheet.)

Logically, to achieve a precise sense of positioning, of differentiation from competitors, their positionings also need to be assessed. Watts defines company positioning thus: 'It has to be more than a slogan. It has to be a description of the company that arises spontaneously if any of its main publics are asked about it.' He demands colourful, apt adjectives rather than bland, knee-jerk phrases like 'quality service'. Everyone claims that.

There could well be a different emphasis to different publics (as long as they don't contradict each other). Every internal activity now has to reflect and build upon the positioning message. Staff at every level need to understand their working purpose in terms of the company's external objectives. The aims are to create relationships (as opposed to sales), manage issues, and concentrate on the opinion formers who influence each public. All communication from now on will reinforce the company's position: all media releases, corporate advertisements, leaflets, annual report commentaries, speeches, briefings, presentations, videos, sponsorship, public statements. 'Remember,' says Watts, 'the objective is to build a lasting relationship with that small band of people who shape the views and attitudes of the other 90 per cent of people working in target audience sector – this may be the market, the local factory communities, or the governmental contacts and specialists.'

A practical project

In their final year on the PR course at Leeds Metropolitan University, students carry out a public relations audit as a group project. Teams of about ten students each work with a medium-sized, local organisation. This is what they do:

- decide what the organisation's goals are
- do a SWOT analysis (strengths, weaknesses, opportunities, threats)
- find out if any of the organisation's activities are against the public interest, or thought to be
- review current public relations activities
- review public relations resources
- look at how the organisation presents itself
- assess how far public relations is integral to the organisation's activities and how far it is treated as a separate specialism
- research internal and external perceptions of the organisation
- decide how promotable the various policies, products and services are
- collect relevant data
- examine training needs
- compare the public relations activities of similar organisations.

This project appears to make the audit structure much wider ranging than Watts' approach but, in fact, most of the activities Leeds students undertake would emerge naturally in a communications audit whose goal was differentiation.

2.5 PR campaign examples

1 HIGH-TECH CASE STUDY

Lesley Fleming of Flora Martin Public Relations in Scotland worked on this nine-month campaign for AutoCAD, a computer-aided design package sold by Academy Design. It shows how public relations can help get the most out of an existing marketing campaign, the value of a strong visual element and central idea, how a launch can be handled without a press conference, the benefit of slanting press releases to individual trade sectors, and the worth of company management talking to journalists to provide direct 'quotes' and additional information.

Objectives

To raise awareness of high-tech company Academy Computers in the general business community and with its main target audiences (designers, architects, engineers and marketing consultants), and to explain what CAD is, and can do.

Background
The client was already spending £100,000 on a 'Designosaurs' marketing campaign, invented by SMARTS Advertising and Design. This had four characters: Mark Etingosaurus, Kong Sultingosaurus, Des Engineerosaurus and Archie Tectosaurus. Direct mail brochures with invitations to free seminars had been prepared. The PR consultant used this campaign as the platform for the PR.

First stage
Absorb information about CAD and talk widely with Academy staff.

Second stage
- Direct photography of life-size cut-outs of the characters
- Write press releases tailored to each market sector
- *Glasgow Herald* business section interview
- Respond to the interest generated.

Third stage
- Send details of individual computer products (StoneMaster, Timber Frame) to trade journals
- Set seminar dates well in advance so these could be publicised through trade journals
- Inform trade associations
- Persuade the client to sponsor the Scottish Joint Contracts Committee's Building Procurement Seminar at the Royal Concert Hall. Attended by engineers, architects and developers from construction companies, who use CAD as a team – using disks not manual drawings. This was ideal for Academy to show a presence, to be seen putting something back into these professions, and to hand out information packs
- Persuade the client to enter the *Glasgow Herald*/Ernst & Young TrailBlazer Awards. They won in the month of November, producing coverage and projecting a quality image
- Enter a business game and Scottish Marketing Awards
- Arrange a lunch meeting between the sales and marketing director and the secretary of the Royal Institute of Architects Scotland
- Arrange a visit by the editor of a London-based CAD magazine to meet Academy directors
- Send out news of staff and customer appointments during the period of the campaign (greater chance of interest).

The sequence of news announcements was:

3 September   Announce the Designosaurs campaign, general release and releases being adapted by each market sector

23 September   Announce the free seminars. £40,000 invested in a seminar suite

22 October   Send out details of new product: CAD Timber Frame for the building industry, and seminar

26 October   Press release on a leasing agreement

20 November   Press release on winning TrailBlazers Award

21 December   Press release on another trade product

20 January   New staff appointment release

24 March   Short article for trade journal.

Costs
From July 1992 to March 1993, consultancy fees, expenses and photography came to £13,000, about an eighth of the advertising and direct mail budget.

Results
From one short piece in *Building* magazine, nearly 50 enquiries. Sales up by a third through the combined PR, sales, marketing and advertising effort. High demand for the seminars – response to the mailings up from 2% to 7% through the introduction of the PR campaign. The project won the IPR Scotland's 1993 Hamp Hamilton award for the best PR project by someone under 25 years of age.

2   LOCAL GOVERNMENT CASE STUDY (BRENT COUNCIL)

This is a summary of the marketing strategy proposed in 1993 for Brent Council (which some still thought of then as 'a loony authority'). It is based on making sure that the product – what the Council does – is sound, and properly communicated to specific publics by each department (or business unit) spending 1% of its budget on marketing. Although the Borough called this a marketing strategy, it is in fact public relations for marketing.

Main public: *The local community* (which pays the salaries)
• Identify the basic services (street cleansing, refuse collection, street care, efficient debt collection, confidence in schools)
• Listen to what the public wants (research)

- Publish clear charters and standards
- Fine tune the service by listening again
- Ensure Brent Council is credited with success.

Other publics: *The Government* (which provides 80% of funds)
- Demonstrate money will be spent wisely, produce well-argued documents
- Use all contacts to lobby decision-makers
- Deliver on promises, build good track record.

Local authorities
- Show how good Brent is by writing in the specialist press, entering awards schemes and speaking at conferences.

The media
- Cut out bad behaviour
- Promote Brent.

(If it takes 20 pieces of good news to counteract one piece of bad news, then if each business unit issues a press release each month – that's 1000 a year from the Council – it would be enough to counteract one piece of bad news each week.)

Members (councillors)
The public goes to councillors with complaints about services rather than to praise. At Brent, the report said, 'The gulf between members and officers is perhaps the most worrying finding of our work.'

- Encourage a greater sense of 'ownership' in councillors
- Provide more open days, facility visits
- Offer more private briefings
- Provide simpler, better information.

Current employees
A satisfied workforce is more likely to produce a quality service and to talk about Brent in a positive way.

- Improve induction and training
- Communicate better
- Improve industrial relations
- Handle people sensitively.

Potential employees
The main way to improve the quality of service is to improve the calibre of staff.

- Be seen as a good employer
- Advertise imaginatively
- Be professional in recruitment
- Have attractive terms and conditions
- Have good coverage in the professional press
- Work at employees speaking well of Brent.

3   CREATIVE CASE STUDY (YORKSHIRE DAY)

Yorkshire Day, 1 August, was started in 1975 by the voluntary organisation, the Yorkshire Ridings Society. The Society feared that the abolition of the Yorkshire Ridings as administrative areas would mean that the original identity of Yorkshire would be lost. After 13 years they felt awareness of Yorkshire Day was low and asked Brahm PR to help, paying a modest fee but offering no funds for promotional material.

Brahm's research confirmed low awareness but revealed great interest. They framed a positioning statement based on Yorkshire pride and set these objectives:

- Identify opportunities that might provide funds for publicity material and be promotional tools in their own right
- Create an infrastructure and a programme of activities
- Allow individuals to take part in Yorkshire Day
- Create a brand identity.

The tactics were:
- Select a local charity as a focal point
- Establish a Yorkshire Day information office at the consultancy's premises, publicised by letter and media briefings
- Design a logo to 'brand' the event
- Hold photocalls (for example, with Fred Trueman)
- Advise members of the Yorkshire Ridings Society on interview technique
- Conduct market research at the Great Yorkshire Show and include light-hearted questions
- Devise plastic white roses to go on cars (like the Comic Relief red noses idea) – people could take part and advertise the project at the same time. Shell sponsored these and their outlets in Yorkshire became distribution points
- Sponsorship arranged with Interflora and Yorkshire Water for posters and Yorkshire Rose buttonholes
- Prevent outsiders feeling left out – have Honorary Yorkshire men

and women; the Yorkshire Building Society branches sold certificates – all receipts to the charity.

They sold 10,000 car roses, took some 350 enquiries at the information office, raised over £15,000 for the Pinderfields Spinal Injuries Centre and, for the first time, generated media coverage ahead of Yorkshire Day itself.

4 YOUTH MARKET CASE STUDY

Public relations can reach niche markets – as in Infopress's work in 1989 for the Britannia Building Society, which wanted to become better known to teenagers.

A national telephone survey of 500 13–18-year-olds had unexpected results:

    78% saved
    Only 26% were told about finance at school
    74% preferred high interest to other incentives
       (record tokens, calculators, etc)
    4% of 13-year-olds were saving for their first home

- Develop story lines
- Aim at media with direct or indirect influence on teenagers
- Press coverage avoided romance and pop stars press. Arranged article, cartoon and competition (generating coverage for the winners) in the 'Indy', then *The Independent*'s junior paper. News release ('Financial Whizz Kids') to the national press. Regional press: South/North differences. Educational press: should financial training be introduced in schools? Women's: ask the children. Financial: humorous release to diary pages of trade press. House journal article.
- Follow-up survey to parents.

The idea was to generate local radio interviews, so Britannia's regional managers were given radio training. The survey information helped in formulating Britannia's 1990–91 marketing strategy, and achieved extensive media coverage.

5 STOCK MARKET CASE STUDY

Ten separate companies were floated on the Stock Exchange in 1989 when the water authorities were privatised. The expected market capitalisation was £5 billion and the cost of the privatisation campaign was never announced. The 1987 stock market crash could have taken away the public's desire for share ownership, the Labour party was ahead of the Conservatives in the polls and, to be a success, all ten companies had to be over-subscribed. Dewe Rogerson handled the communication campaign directed at the following publics:

- Investors (UK institutions, the public, overseas institutions, employees)
- Influencers: the media and the brokers' analysts
- Advisers: intermediaries such as accountants, solicitors, stock-brokers, bank managers
- The political and environmental lobbies.

The strategy was:
- Create a feeling of scarcity
- Focus on the business aspects of the ten companies
- Have the merchant bank, not politicians, as the main spokespeople so that the issue would not be seen as political
- Release information gradually to build up to a climax when the price was decided
- Control the messages centrally to ensure consistency and clarity.

The tactics were:
- The H_2O design style as a corporate identity
- Print and information sheets
- Share information office to handle enquiries and send out information packs and prospectuses
- Direct mail (to 20 million people)
- Information for intermediaries
- Roadshow presentations
- National and regional media relations
- Employee communications
- Video, for the roadshows
- Advertisements.

THE WATER
SHARE OFFERS

Research was done at the start and tracking research continued through the campaign. All ten offers were over-subscribed, there were 2.7 million applications and £7 billion was invested.

2.6 Measurement and evaluation

Measuring results and evaluating them have begun to be preoccupations of PR. The reasons are several. Rather like the groundswell to pick up on BS 5750, ANSI/ASQC/Q90 and Quality processes, evaluation is something you have to introduce because others are using it. This makes their work more professional than yours. Somehow, it becomes expected. In the background all the time is PR's need to demonstrate its worth to management, to be subject to the kind of criteria that define highly regarded disciplines. That the client or managing director is satisfied seems no longer to be enough. In many cases, particularly for small organisations, it is enough. Whoever you are working with will have their own reasons for using PR; you may not even be aware of them. You might be unwise to push evaluation down their throat. That could be seen as an unwelcome criticism or an unnecessary expense. Be content that they are pleased with their 'PR'.

A good relationship with your client or boss is worth more than clinical calculation of the (often) meaningless. The time, effort and budget spent unnecessarily trying to prove a point could be better expended on more forward-looking projects. The dedicated cuttings evaluation services cost between £300 and £1000 to examine 200 cuttings a month. For some small companies £4000 to £12,000 a year could be better spent on hiring a freelance public relations consultant and not measuring what they do. Heretical? Not in the real terms of running small businesses. After all, if you are knowledgeable and experienced, and management makes the judgement that you know what you are doing, what's the point in checking up on small-time results? Many a PR campaign may have been only partially successful against pre-set targets, but what of all the extra benefits that are discovered along the way?

Management is supposed to believe that if you can't measure public relations then it's not worth doing. Modern management, which seems to live by setting targets and proving itself in relation to them, might think that; it's doubtful if most successful entrepreneurs do. Unless thinking that public relations is a good thing is what is meant by measurement.

A 1993 survey of the responses of 259 practitioners in membership of the IPR (a thousand were mailed a questionnaire) found that many viewed evaluation very narrowly, feared it as a challenge to their advice and activities, and lacked time, budget and knowledge of how to do it. Easily the most common reason for evaluation was to prove the value of a campaign or of budget expenditure. This is a largely self-justifying motive compared with using evaluation techniques as a guide to improving a programme or judging its effects and consequences.

Tom Watson, managing director of Hallmark Marketing Services, carried out the survey as part of his postgraduate studies at Southampton University. He found that of eight speciality areas of public relations, media relations/publicity was the most frequently checked; then corporate image/identity and marketing/product PR. Investor/financial relations was the least evaluated sector. His finding was that practitioners did not spend money on formal evaluation; if they did it was to justify themselves rather than to improve programmes; but over half had great hopes for the development of applied measures just using software. Evaluation of the simplest kind was done by some 62% of respondents – mainly a review by the project manager. Reasons given for not using evaluation included: lack of time, of budget and of information about methods. 'They also feared evaluation,' wrote Tom Watson, 'because it could challenge the logic of their advice and activities. Yet they think public relations suffers because of the inability to predict and measure results . . . There seems to be a simple faith in the power of the PC to add value to PR activity.' He reported that the methods most likely to have been used were 'output measures such as monitoring media for coverage and keeping clippings files'.

Dr Jon White divides evaluation into objective and subjective measures. Objective include change in behaviour, degree of response, shift in awareness and opinion, ratings of media coverage, campaign reach, and distribution (of information). Subjective measures include client satisfaction (which some PR people believe is the best measure of all), respected judgement, intuition and gut feeling. He believes that all managers work by hunch and feel, and that those in PR are no different. ('I've just managed it even though I can't measure it'.) It all depends, of course, on what you mean by evaluation.

Judging award winners

Awards schemes, prolific in public relations, do increase the likelihood that programmes will have built-in evaluation criteria. The IPR's Sword of Excellence Awards, for instance, set a strict structure for entries: information, planning, action, measurement. These four elements are fundamental to public relations campaigns. If you have no means of evaluating the result, better not enter the competition. Public relations case study competitions include evaluation partly because that encourages measurement to be a constant part of PR thinking, partly because competition judges need criteria. The chairman of the judges in 1993, Professor Robert Worcester of MORI, explained why submissions were not shortlisted: 'Some entries never had a hope, failing to demonstrate any strategic purpose for their being. Others failed to suggest why the campaign had been launched or gave no evidence of any evaluation other than that "the client liked it".' This is where competitions differ from real life.

Analysing 40 category winners from the last six years of entries in the Sword of Excellence confirms Tom Watson's finding that media coverage is by far the most common criterion. Once or twice it is summed up in terms of Opportunities to See (OTS) or 'reach' or Advertising Value Equivalent (AVE). More often the entries simply record the extent and variety of coverage. Here is a typical extract: 'New Fish on the Block secured massive coverage in all sectors of consumer media. Highlights included TV-AM, Food and Drink Programme (BBC 2), Steve Wright In The Afternoon (BBC Radio 1), Jimmy Young Show (BBC Radio 2), Chris Tarrant (Capital Radio), *Daily Star, Daily Telegraph, Best, Woman's Realm* and 48 regional radio stations. The campaign generated 92,869,739 opportunities to see (cumulative readership, viewing and listening figures). Quality of coverage was high with an average of two of the three agreed consumer messages being delivered in each item.'

Advertising Value Equivalent is frequently quoted. For the Lynx Public Relations entry on Vauxhall's Womens' Institute Woman Driver of the Year competition in 1990: 'Editorial space and radio airtime at advertising rates was valued at over £250,000, excluding television air time. This takes no account of the theory that editorial credibility enhances its space value over advertising by a factor of three.'

Measuring the cost of editorial in terms of advertising rates, frowned on for decades by purists, is now being forced into the arena by the constant demand for evaluation and, of course, because management likes 'numbers'. But its use brings media coverage too close to being 'free advertising', an impression practitioners have fought against for years. AVE is entirely hypothetical because no such sums would have been spent, nor could have been spent, on editorial coverage. Similarly dubious is the idea that editorial is three (or five or eight) times more valuable than advertising. Studies on this are hard to come by. It is based on the premise that in an advertisement you say what you want yourself but if a journalist says it for you, as a third party, it has been filtered through editorial scrutiny and therefore can be better trusted.

The second most common method of evaluation in the winning entries from the Sword of Excellence competition was research. By establishing the position at the start of a campaign you set up a 'benchmark'. Conducting matching research during the campaign and when it is over allows you to measure a shift (always assuming the research is representative). The shift in tracking research might be in opinion, intent, awareness, behaviour; or it could be numerical. A third of the winners used this technique. It is more often found in campaigns where there is sufficient budget to pay for before-and-after or before-during-and-after studies. Not all programmes, however, have a beginning and an end. Research can run year on year, monitoring trends so that action can be taken where attitudes or behaviour have shifted. The simplest form of measurement is to set objectives at the beginning and see how well you have met them when the campaign is complete. This is open to abuse if the objectives set are too easy or unrealistic – and in competitions if they are invented after the event.

The Manchester 2000 bid for the Olympics failed, losing to Sydney. But the value of its momentum to the city and the north-west of England was significant.

Achieving a specific objective can be the sole criterion of success and this is common with political campaigns. Thus with the Learn and Live parents' campaign for safe driving tuition, and the British Pest Control campaign to abolish Crown immunity (which used to protect hospitals from prosecution under the food and hygiene regulations). The campaigns were successful because the law and the regulations were changed as a result.

Budget has to be taken into account in judging success. A quarter of the campaigns emphasised that they met or were within budget, or expended only a relatively small sum as a measure. But how do you compare a stock market flotation with a huge budget against creative miracles worked on a shoe-string? One campaign – for garden gnomes – gained amazing coverage for only a few hundred pounds because the media loved it (gnomes marching across the Pennines, gnomes chaining themselves to the railings at the Chelsea Flower Show).

The big City flotations and privatisations have been measured by the number of times the shares were over-subscribed, internal relations by employee understanding and reaction, product campaigns by sales or enquiries. Each public relations sector has its own natural and often obvious criteria.

A measure may be the absence of something. The lack of complaints about the British Gas North Thames pipeline across Hampstead Heath. The way tobacco tax was fended off more years than not, partly as a result of the long-running campaign by Edelman PR Network for the retailers of the Tobacco Alliance. The ultimate measure of success for some media campaigns is that nothing is published: a story is kept out of the media.

Sometimes the number of awards a project has already won are given as a measure. Much depends on the nature of the campaign and the PR sector it is in.

The most obvious measure is there all the time if objectives are set beforehand. Any awards scheme judge will look at the objectives set and see how well they were met; at the top of the scale this is one way of separating the outstanding entries from the merely very good. Privately, any sensible client will do the same against his own objectives (which just maybe you do not know about).

All the time there is an uncomfortable feeling that evaluation is being done to promote public relations, to justify consultancy spend, to claim that it's only 'proper' PR if it is measured. But it is a tide that will be impossible to resist, like the European Union.

Expectations of PR

In Gillian Hogg's 1993 survey for Stirling University of purchasers' expectations of PR from in-house departments and consultancies in Scotland, over half the respondents were happy with human judgement and 'feel good' reactions; less than half used any type of formal evaluation. Cost is the initial problem. The Scottish survey showed no correlation between expenditure and evaluation under £100,000. Public relations campaigns cost far less than advertising. Modest budgets from £5000 to £30,000 a year make up much normal expenditure. There is little room for the cost of tracking research in these. Many of the small budget campaigns are the most inventive and creative. You don't need anything more than intuition to see that. It would often be much better to spend the extra money on more public relations activities. Or give time to helping clients and bosses understand what public relations is. With that trust they would not feel the need to spend money on unnecessary evaluation. Big budget programmes, on the other hand, can afford to do it properly. Evaluation can then become a justification for the cost – as long as the results are good, of course. With the money spent on some of the big privatisation campaigns in the 1980s, some form of justification was needed.

SOME WAYS OF EVALUATING PRESS COVERAGE

– the number of cuttings, articles, mentions
– the number of words
– single column centimetres (scc)

– position on the page, in the publication
– size and position of photograph
– dominance and accuracy of headline

– relevance of publication

– circulation, readership, opportunities to see (OTS)
– cost in advertising terms (AVE)

– favourable, unfavourable or neutral coverage
– main points included
– influence on attitudes and behaviour

Dermot McKeone, Infopress

Measuring media coverage

A new business has grown up with specialist companies competing in offering services for media evaluation. Here the distinction is marked between quantitative measures – the computer-counted number of, volume of, size of this or that – as against qualitative measures – where human judgement evaluates in the more sophisticated terms of, say, the tone of comment, the degree of understanding or fairness. Some measures are primitive, even trivial. The results are often a matter of chance. The only control you have over editorial coverage is the quality of the material you provide; you can't otherwise influence the size of a photograph, the length of a story, the page it appears on. Not if journalists are self-respecting and competent and refuse to allow the relationship with you to interfere with their objective judgement.

According to Dermot McKeone, managing director of Infopress Communications, one of the companies specialising in media evaluation, there are two essentials to analyse (in addition to the volume of coverage). The text should include the messages you have agreed you want to get across; the media should be appropriate to your target publics. He sees media evaluation reports on an organisation's involvement – or not – in issues such as the environment, as an important contribution to management strategy and planning. 'Responsible management,' he says, 'receiving negative messages each month from a media analysis report, will act to attack the problem that is causing negative messages to appear.' McKeone sees media evaluation reports as a PR stick with which to beat on management's door. If the competition is doing better, there's an argument for greater PR spend (or firing the present staff). If agreed messages are getting through then the PR programme is on the right course. If the comments about the company are negative,

---

TYPICAL USES OF PRESS COVERAGE ANALYSIS

– finding out the true reasons for adverse publicity

– assessing the impact of editorial coverage on a particular audience

– seeing how image compares with that of a competitor

– spotting bias in specific journalists' relationships with companies, financial analysts

– building up patterns on how individual journalists operate

– creating an early warning system to highlight issues discussed in the media

– measuring which issues gain most attention from a particular media segment

– comparing the incidence of PR-generated coverage with unsolicited coverage

– measuring the relative press exposure gained by different company executives.

(Uses listed by CARMA)

---

management can be presented with the evidence and perhaps persuaded to alter course. If that is achieved, it is pure public relations.

In his book *Evaluating Press Coverage*, David Phillips (who runs Media Measurement) details how the computer can be used to relate share of coverage with sales enquiries, to track competitors' coverage and compare it with your own, to analyse coverage by publication, by journalist, and by many other computations.

CARMA (Computer Aided Research and Media Analysis) has carried out studies in which researchers evaluate content and turn it into graphics and charts to aid management decision-making. They can identify the attitudes of individual journalists and put them on disk so that, when a journalist rings, you can call up details on your PC screen of his past approach to your company. They can identify and tabulate patterns in volumes of coverage which management would never read.

2.7 Guiding principles

A crucial point about journalism was made by John Tusa, then managing director of the BBC World Service, in a lecture to the Thomson Foundation in September 1992. He was speaking against a background of constant public and government criticism of journalism.

First he quoted a *British Journalism Review* editorial which argued that authority sets out to protect and reinforce its concept of what it believes to be the best interests of the nation. 'If that means concealment, "black information", fabrication, exaggerated complaints against press "neutrality", then so be it. Authority will gladly live with that. The journalist cannot.' When the journalists start asking questions, however, the critics of the media then ask who gave the journalists the right to behave as they do. Tusa's answer: 'The media have no choice but to ask questions of the government of the day or the state of the moment, not because they are special, not because they are arrogant, not because they are self-appointed, but because *if they do not do it, nobody else will.*' He was referring to the highest levels of public information ('Many are the enemies of free information lying in wait for us throughout the world') but what he says holds true across the board. Later in his lecture, discussing the attributes of a good journalist, he said: 'You must be curious about ideas, and be sceptical of briefings, official handouts, steers, spin, and all partial presentation of the facts.' And 'ultimately, the definition of good, responsible journalism lies in its connection with and reflection of reality.'

Organisations, especially businesses, similarly protect and reinforce their concept of what they believe to be in their own best interests. The journalist will be equally sceptical of them. There is no argument but that public relations, unless it has to do otherwise, gives a particular version of the facts. Most organisations have dark facts locked away; facts of which you will be ignorant. The real intent will be concealed in the short if not the long term, mission statement or not. It cannot be otherwise without giving away plans and tactics to competitors, or putting ultimate, probably secret, ambitions at risk.

The organisation wants to be the one to set the agenda for what is known. That means that for any information being given out or for any questions asked, its PR department must control the communication agenda. But journalism also wants to set the agenda, not only to ferret out the truth but for the sake of a 'good story' and to sell newspapers. Journalists question motives, cast doubt, throw up unrealised facts. At the tabloid end of the press this becomes simplistic, entertaining – and sensationalised. At the broadsheet end, with the quality papers, there is much background analysis. Both approaches have disturbing consequences for management because they do not want to lose control, as they may with an ill-thought-out speech, a poor performance on television, a bad radio interview.

One way of controlling the agenda is to broaden it, introduce aspects you want discussed or known. Another is to reduce the flow of information on what you see as the negative side and increase it on what is, to you, the positive side. Another is to influence the thinking. 'Negative' (bad) and 'positive' (good) thoughts are strong influencers of the agenda. If you are in any of the promotional disciplines you are not encouraged to be negative – only positive. Negative is thought to damage the organisation, reduce morale, present competitors with weak points to take advantage of. Positive, on the other hand, is in favour of the organisation, so that's OK. As, on this basis, the organisation is unlikely to be self-critical, management needs somehow or other to examine its soul before it takes all these positive actions. One PR function is to be part of management's conscience.

The scope of public relations in an organisation, how far it is able to look into the soul of management and do something about what it sees, depends entirely on how close to the power centre the top people in public relations are. If PR is an accepted management function at the highest level, then public relations will have real control over the agenda in the public domain. Current developments make that more likely and more common. First is the communications revolution. Second is the rise of environmental causes and pressure groups of all kinds (the first concentrates management attention and the second demonstrates the concerted use of public relations in, generally, 'good' causes. Third is the so-called change management culture shifts that have been absorbing the commercial world, with their emphasis on teams, quality, flat organisation and workforce motivation. Management discovers the importance of good internal public relations. All this suggests that public relations thinking and attitudes, with their emphasis on reputation, understanding and credibility, now have more natural acceptance among those who run organisations.

Principles of public relations thinking

Always bear the following guiding principles in mind.

1 *Declare your interest*   It is intrinsic to professional public relations that the source of all its messages and activities should be known and declared.

2 *Fitting the organisation's purpose and aims*   If you run a small business you will know precisely what you want to achieve. If you are a manager in a large company you will have a tight brief. If you are a consultant you will have absorbed what your clients' work is and realise when some action or project is inappropriate. Always ask: in what ways will the work I am doing help the organisation? You do not want to spend time on unnecessary projects, ones that are perhaps easy to do, impressive even, but which waste resources through not being related to policy. You could be better employed; the organisation could be better served.

It is much better to query the wisdom of a brief than to carry it out without thinking. You do not need to be thought to be questioning management's ability (a dangerous approach) but simply clarifying what is expected of you (I am asked to prepare a release which says management is not to blame – but what if it is?). Any brief should make clear statements about objectives and programme.

Public relations projects also have a habit of running away with themselves as creative ideas take over. This momentum creates further demands on time and money; before you know where you are, you are communicating madly but are not sure why. Every action and activity should relate to objectives in the brief. Sometimes bosses think it is a good idea to make a speech, get an article in the press, write to their MP, hold a reception. But your public relations instincts may tell you they may only be feeding their own egos. You need to be sure there are valid reasons.

Essentially, you need to understand both your organisation's aims and the current thinking in the world outside and around it. Match the two, and pinpoint the variance. Then decide what public relations needs to do in that context to serve the organisation's aims or to change them.

3   *Think through to the possible consequences*   Part of your job – and easier sometimes than querying the brief if you are in a junior position – is to judge the likely consequences. Top people do not necessarily think these through. They believe they have an opportunity to impress and they may well take it for its own sake. One of the attributes of some bosses is a tunnel-vision view of their own indestructibility, their ability to control events. You, in your less exalted role, may be able to see that it could be more trouble than it is worth. Is their supposed crusade for the environment just a way of making sales, and will it be seen as that? Does it matter? Make a simple analysis of likely benefits in relation to costs.

Have they gauged their audience right; do they really have the support they think; will a speech simply open them up to criticism? Will the journalist interview turn out as they expect or could it back-fire, with lots of awkward questions on some other subject? When *The Times* cut its price shortly before the first move was made in the Kasparov v Short world championship chess match in 1993 which it was sponsoring, the editor of the paper introduced the players but then left the stage. This kept the one topic away from the other.

Consequences come in other forms than audience backlash. The cost may be too great. Resources may be too stretched. Competitors may be alerted well before necessary. The organisation's reputation may suffer. The actions may not further management's objectives at all. You will often find that after a bout of robust, polite, ingenuous questioning, the tactics change. Frequently, when written material is involved – a report, a press release, a speech – the experience of seeing their thoughts expressed accurately in writing produces a change in plan. Similarly, many keen to appear on television have second thoughts when they see themselves in training sessions. Something else will come up which has precedence.

4 *Do not make assumptions* This means avoiding having your information at second hand. Always check back, always check up, both internally and externally. At some point you have to trust your staff – but only if they have the same 'check' mentality. However hard you work at checking, something will still be wrong. So imagine how badly things could go if you do not check at all.

Equally, be certain what your brief is, that you have read or listened to it carefully and not misunderstood. People can be accidentally ambiguous with language: what they say is not necessarily what they thought they said, nor what you hear. Hours, days, weeks even can be saved by being certain you are doing what is expected; or if you decide to do something better, that it is wanted. Make sure, too, that your brief is from the right person. This is one sterling argument for writing up working notes and circulating them widely. The reaction from one recipient might show you have been misled.

5 *Research the background* Researching the background to a task or project is logically connected to not making assumptions but it can go a lot further. Research can be quite basic. You may only need to do some desk research, talk to people, make a few phone calls, look up some documents, to orientate yourself and be sure of working from a sound platform. When you are thinking about a public relations project you cannot afford to come across surprise information too late on. (Why didn't you tell me . . . ? Sorry, I didn't think.) You may also need to turn to research more formally. This may be benchmark research to establish the position at the start of a campaign, so that further research at the end can be used as a measure or guide for future activity.

In public relations, market research can be used to decide how the organisation's PR should be directed – what publics are concerned; or to measure the effectiveness of a campaign; or to supply new information about some product or action.

6 *Have clear objectives* If you can be clear on what you need to achieve – sales of a certain level, a percentage increase in awareness, contact with new publics, bringing about a change of rules or the law – then it is much easier to run a campaign dedicated to achieving that specific objective. And, as long as you are able to measure, you will have no trouble arguing success. You will be

able to think much more clearly if you have specific objectives that are concise and measurable. You will not need to worry about tangential programmes and will find you can more readily dismiss activities that might otherwise have seemed attractive. When the whole universe of possibilities is open to you it is far harder to plan than if you have only a few options.

Don't let people pressure you into aiming at the unattainable. Agree to what is realistic. Don't let the objectives be too vague either; that makes thinking difficult and evaluation impossible. Don't be afraid of challenging the objectives if they seem to you to be unobtainable. Try to pin them down: with luck, that will help clarify the thoughts of those who drew up the brief. Geographically, where exactly? On what budget? Who or what is the target? How long have you got? How many people can work on the assignment? Practical questions quickly change objectives.

7 *Think as specifically as possible about relationships* You will find it impossible to think about communicating with the general public (even though that is how public relations got its name) without breaking down this abstract into concrete, definable sections. Otherwise you will never know who you are talking to and so won't be able to communicate with them except incompletely and by chance. The likelihood of feedback will be remote and if there is a response it won't be statistically relevant.

When the technology of mass communication first came about through the popular press, wireless and the early days of television, there was a greater sense of influencing the public as a whole, as in war. Today, there is a vast range of media serving an ever more diverse society. People are more able to choose what they want to hear. Perhaps because they are selling harder, specialists in advertising, marketing and direct mail divide people up into smaller and smaller groups with common characteristics and interests. This narrowing of marketing targets, and the computer technology that can pin-point geodemographically, intensifies the same approach in defining publics. Within ostensibly similar groups (say shareholders) are age and lifestyle differences that could need taking into account. Not only do publics overlap (just as the same people represent more than one public) but within any one public may be further subdefinable groups. The more you concentrate on a specific group the more successful your communication is likely to be. Smaller groups increase the likelihood of more personal contact (never better, of course, than one to one and face to face).

8 *Use as many channels as possible*   Usually, if you hear something from an expected source it has less influence than if it comes at you from all directions. Repetition is part of the explanation, credibility another. With indirect media – newspapers, radio, magazines – someone has to select what you will learn about. In today's jargon they are 'gatekeepers', letting information through, or not, as they deem suitable for their audiences (or their advantage). If they consider information worth passing on then it has more weight, more value because of that. Hence the 'silly season' in the media during August when there is traditionally more trivial news than normal: much the same space and time to fill but the news and the newsmakers seem to have gone on holiday. Through longer holiday entitlements, Christmas to mid-January is now also a slow news period.

The sheer weight of communication at any one time also makes the message seem important. Such intensity partly explains the frequent success of flotations on the stock market and the privatisation programmes of the UK Conservative government. Suddenly it seems everyone is doing it, we mustn't miss out. The herd instinct is powerful, as with the Prudential's decision in 1985 to buy estate agencies, stampeding other financial service companies to do the same and soon reaping losses all round. Information being reinforced through a radio programme here, a direct mail shot there, a chance remark from a friend, an argument in a pub, a newspaper story, the results of research, both maintains awareness and influences opinion. A variety of approaches creates continuity, consistency and credibility.

Your ultimate task is to choose the right messages, send them to the right audiences, through the right means of communication.

9 *Make sure your messages are consistent*   If you tell your employees one thing, your customers another and your shareholders yet another, you are asking for trouble. If you are not consistent from public to public, people will begin to doubt your veracity and lose confidence. They will think they see a vacillating, unethical, uncoordinated organisation. You will lose the benefits of reinforcing the same messages. Publics overlap: your customer may be your employee and your shareholder. This is not to say that you should avoid stressing different aspects to different

publics to emphasise their special interests. They should not, however, contradict each other. It is easy for business people to fall into the trap of not seeing that a benefit to one group can be a disadvantage to another. Putting up your prices will be disliked by customers but probably applauded by shareholders.

10 *Approach different publics in and on their own terms* This seems to be the most obvious thing in the world but is often not practicable. Budget is partly the limitation; arrogance, thoughtlessness and laziness are other causes. Marketing has many lessons for public relations in this respect. Communication that works with children is unlikely to work with the over-50s. Publications for young women are rarely read by older women. The readers of the *Sun* will not often be seen reading the *Economist* (although in the days of strong unions the workforce was hot on the *Financial Times*, where they might well find business messages that conflicted with what employees understood). People who take life in visually will not trouble with three-page letters to shareholders.

If you want to sell a product you stress the benefits that mean most to the particular prospect. Some may buy on price, others on elegance, still others on functionality. Unless you are to be your brother's keeper your job is to sell the product, not to 'correct' the perceptions of the buyer. If you are unable to talk in the language of the publics you are reaching out to, then keep your language and your messages clear and simple, without being patronising. Send messages that anyone can understand.

11 *Think through everything – be prepared* The only way to be sure you can answer all the questions you may be asked after making a presentation is to have anticipated what they will be. If you have not done that you have not thought through your subject properly. Uncertainty leaves you vulnerable to critics and makes supporters uneasy. The same is true of the entire public relations field. The process is at its most obvious in those question and answer sessions at rehearsals for press conferences. You try to think of the worst question the most inquisitive journalist present could ask. This is also a devious way that you, as organiser, can get through to your boss or client a weakness that you might find it awkward to discuss with them otherwise. As you are supposed to be the communication expert you will probably find yourself having to phrase the definitive reply.

If you are working on a written programme, work through every step: likely ramifications, practicalities, timings, availability. Does it make sense? Will it work? Is there time? If you are running an event, go through the whole thing in your head, talk it through with somebody, break it down into sequences. If something can be rehearsed, rehearse. Think about the reactions of others, especially your opponents. What will they do? If that, then what? Can you take the risk?

In your dealings with people you must develop a sixth sense that tells you when to be wary. Others will prepare against you; you must prepare for what they have in store for you. Keep the facts and figures handy that are to do with things that matter. If you haven't got them, don't trust to luck; go out of your way to obtain them if at all possible. If you have a poor memory, write everything down, learn it; make lists. Always ask yourself: what am I likely to be asked, what could go wrong, have I got an answer?

All this preparation will do wonders for your self-confidence because it will test how good your plan is and give you time to change it.

12 *Be ethical, and do not lie* Follow the IPR's code of professional conduct and make sure that all your dealings with people are fair.

You do not have to tell the whole truth but be sure that what you do say is true and does not mislead.

Upon these two characteristics depend both your self-regard and your credibility as a public relations practitioner.

In their book, *Goodbye to the Low Profile*, Herb Schmertz and William Novak talk of the art of creative confrontation. Their principles are:

- Grab the good words and concepts for yourself – use emotional language
- Don't be predictable – let them worry about what you may do
- In debate, go first, because you can set the agenda
- Show your thought process, not just your conclusions – explaining can change minds
- Know when you've lost – you can't win 'em all. Cut your losses.

2.8 PR then and now

In late 1930s Britain, the idea of the study of relations with the public, analysing publics and defining public attitudes was just beginning as a discipline. After the Second World War (a time when it is hard to disassociate propaganda from public relations) the working definition of PR was that you did PR if you didn't buy advertising space. Probably two-thirds of PR counselling was in the hands of advertising agencies. During the 1950s and 60s advertising agencies would set up PR departments whose responsibilities in the beginning were to seek 'free editorial' for their advertising clients.

The birth of the business news sections in the quality nationals in the late 1950s and early 1960s opened up the press to industry. Financial and business news was written up by journalists, many of whom later moved into PR departments or into consultancies (for more money) and began specialising in City and financial public relations. They knew how newspapers worked, how business and financial affairs worked and, having been on the receiving end, how press relations worked. They were valuable people for consultancies to have advising boards of directors.

It is no different today when a specialist from financial services, health, stockbroking, accountancy or the law joins a PR consultancy to use their specialist knowledge on behalf of clients. As businesses expanded in the 1960s they began to merge by agreement or after contested takeover bids. Much new PR work accrued from this. Once you had learned how to handle one takeover, you became an expert. Clients came to you because you had done it before. As these companies became bigger, many of them turning into conglomerates, their internal and external communication necessarily became more complex and many needed sizeable in-house public relations departments and consultancy help.

Parallel with this came the problems of handling their international communications. UK boards of directors still favoured hierarchical structures for management but were becoming curious about Japanese success.

From the 1950s, mainframe computers began playing an increasing part in providing information for business but until the development of the desk top personal computer (PC) information was a fairly centralised possession.

The trade unions had, until the late 1980s, a grip on working practices. It took management a long time to realise that they did not have to use union representatives to communicate with their workforces. They could go direct and control the message. At one time it was the trades union representatives who did well on television while rather old hat, public-school-sounding British management seemed unprepared. Television training only then became a habit for leading business people and MPs. The trades union guide to using the media – and it meant *using* the media – is an instructive read.

From the 1960s to 1980s public relations grew in dimension, but patchily. The Government Information Services saw, and still see, themselves as informing, not persuading. Some local authorities used PROs but they had an uphill struggle. The public services sector – from the police to the National Health Service – only gradually came to terms with professional communication in relations with the public.

There is now much more specialisation of public relations skills. The work has moved from being the province of the generalist to being broken down by specialism. Clients want consultancies who already know about their type of business; in-house PR departments and consultancies recruit staff who already have specialised knowledge, either of a business sector (hi-tech, consumer goods, food and nutrition for instance) or of a particular aspect of public relations (such as lobbying, audio/visual, internal communication, crisis PR or investor relations).

For those who wanted public relations to have greater stature, the emphasis was too often on what they call technical skills – running events, writing and editing, making films, arranging exhibitions – than taking part in formulating an organisation's strategy and planning. That has been the bane of the careers of many senior professional PR people; they don't want to be just the messengers, nor do they want simply to help write the message. They want to be part of the decision that there should be a message. Financial PR people claimed for a long time that they wanted to do more than sit outside the boardroom door waiting to be given a company's half-year figures to take round to the Stock Exchange. Tim Traverse-Healy, 1994/5 visiting professor at Stirling University, said at a PR congress in 1986 that he wanted to be an architect, not an artisan.

Part of the problem has been the calibre of the people in the PR business, looked at from a purely management and management training perspective. Although there were many capable heads of public relations and, latterly, directors of corporate communication, they rarely have seats on the main board. Either communication isn't important enough to sit alongside finance, production and human resources, or management doesn't see, in PR, people like themselves. However, since the early 1980s – which shows how long it takes for new ideas to percolate through – changes have been taking place which should put public relations and communication skills at the centre of organisational survival:

1   The technological revolution of electronics (and optics) is completely changing the conduits of communication. You need to monitor developments continually.

2   Information technology (IT) is providing almost more information than people can cope with. Through PCs, soon to be as common as the telephone, everyone can share information. The information superhighway will soon be jammed with traffic; and you need to be there. For example, Internet, the worldwide chat-and-information electronic network, means everyone can be your neighbour now.

    Since 1984, public relations people have had their own virtual community, the Public Relations Interest Group (now with 20,000 members), through subscribing to CompuServe. A similar service, PRFORUM, started on Internet in 1994.

3   The convergence of computers, publishing and TV/video is creating new media – including the multi-media of interactive CD disk systems – and altering the way people learn (bringing 'edutainment' to the masses).

4   Communication has speeded up and broadened what you can do when you are communicating. All you need when travelling is a laptop computer and a telephone/modem plug in your hotel room and your information is back to base. All you need on the train is a mobile telephone and it's as if you never went away. As the cost of technology comes down so even teleconferencing will become quite normal. With videophones the pet cat of the telemuter working from home will be on screen. Keep up to date.

5   Satellites and cable TV are breaking up the formal broadcasting establishments and offering innumerable new channels of communication. The rules over sponsoring programmes have weakened. The shotgun of mass communications through few press, radio and television channels is giving way to the rifleshot of hun-

dreds of fragmented, separate broadcast channels with their inevitably smaller but more homogeneous audiences.

6   The 1987–92 recession jolted businesses into scaling down their organisations, making redundancies, defining their core businesses, learning about change management and delayering (removing middle management and replacing many of them with intelligent computers). Now companies are 'flatter', with key people nearer the customer. This has made a business out of internal communication counselling.

7   Organisations are becoming more collaborative in order to survive and prosper. Partnerships with suppliers and sponsors are the business way forward. You must come up with ideas.

8   The environmental movement, championed by Greenpeace, Friends of the Earth and many more, confronted industry in the 1970s and 1980s. They challenged the pollution caused by manufacturers, unethical behaviour, markets based on mistreating animals. The Body Shop made a business out of 'Green'. Now there is environmental auditing. The importance of thinking aɔout the effects of what organisations do could not be more clear.

9   Organisations are having to come to terms with their social responsibilities. While power may be in the hands of the big corporations to shape trading in the way best for them, the pressures today are strong on business to put back into, and not damage, the society which it needs, serves and uses. Community relations are on the agenda; and sponsorship; and synergistic alliances. Altruism rarely, not even in fund raising.

10 New cultures in the country have brought new problems for communicators to solve, new groups of people to reach. Communicating with minorities is a new speciality.

11 New company cultures are being built, bed-rocked in customer service and listening. They have mission, they have values. They have BS 5750 in Britain, EN 29002 in Europe, ISO 9002 internationally and ANSI/ASQC Q90 in the States. Some even have Total Quality Management. They have customer service charters, their employees have empowerment. Their managers are accountable and seek value added and added value. Measurement and evaluation are new public relations gods, for without these, it is thought, management can never be convinced

of PR's worth. Corporate culture has numerous other devices which bleep: 'We are different now'. Meanwhile disgruntled minicab drivers (recently redundant business executives) say it's the same as 20 years ago, except the words are different. As Peter Middleton, chief executive of Lloyd's of London said: 'There are fashions in what management teams should do that circulate every 20 years or so, with due changes in terminology. I tell you, Quality circles are coming round again. Just in a different form.' A veritable communication feast here, with the prospect of it all being done again. Change management consultants say change hasn't worked.

12 Marshall McLuhan's 1970s forecast of the global village is with us. Other people's wars and disasters become ours every morning on the Today programme and breakfast TV. Jet travel, fax, telephone, satellite are just some of the forces shaking us into awareness of other cultures, other people's problems that all pour into the communication soup. Current affairs is no longer an occasional school lesson; it is perpetual and a proper subject for day-to-day PR study. Listen, watch and learn, even if you do not enjoy what you hear.

13 The Conservative Government's 15-year push for an American-style society, based on independence and the ability to pay, has broken up most public sector institutions into privatised services. They all need public relations. And if a Labour Government changed it all back again, *it* would need public relations.

14 Europe is in the grip of political and economic change with, on the one hand, the effects of being suddenly in a Single Market and, on the other, the collapse of communism in Eastern Europe, coupled with the reunification of Germany. European PR networks are licking their lips while more and more consultants are flying to the new countries of the east, who are eager to learn both capitalism and public relations.

Each of these changes would be threatening to the old way of life on its own. Together they are deadly to the past, which they suck dry of what little juice is left and then spit out the irrelevant bits like a golden eagle digests the flesh of a young bird before disgorging claws, beak and gristle in one neat, disposable ball. The old way of life is changed irrevocably. The opportunities it creates for ethical public relations practitioners are manifest and manifold.

2.9   Ethics and law

Ethics

If you are a manager and are looking for someone who can put one over on the public, don't bother trying to employ a member of the Institute of Public Relations. If you are interested in taking a job in public relations because you are good at deception and dissimulation, don't even think about it – not if you want to qualify for membership of the Institute. Some able and honourable PR people are not members of the Institute and are guided by their own consciences, and, in some cases, by the ethical stance of their organisations. On the other hand, the majority of serious practitioners are now members of the IPR and work within the constraints of its code of professional conduct. That code is backed up by a complaints procedure handled through the IPR's Professional Practices Committee. When there is a serious suspicion that a member is flouting the code of conduct, the case will be passed to the IPR's Disciplinary Committee. Sanctions include reprimand, suspension or dismissal from the Institute.

Any member of the public and any organisation can make a complaint against an IPR member as can other IPR members, its other committees or its Council. The code is available from the IPR with an interpretation of each of its clauses. Members are expected to be familiar with its rules and the changes that are occasionally made to keep it in step with the times. The code's aim is to 'make for good relationships and reputable business dealing by public relations practitioners'. Thus it controls conduct in four areas: the general practice of public relations; fair dealings with the public, the media, and other professional people; employers and clients; and colleagues.

If you have a strong conscience the main injunctions will come as no surprise. In brief, members must:

• Observe the highest standards of practice, dealing fairly and honestly with their own and their organisations' publics
• Make sure their staff, whether IPR members or not, act within the code
• Behave well, without detriment to the public relations profession or the Institute
• Have proper regard for the public interest
• Keep to the truth, check all information before putting it out, and make sure it is neither false nor misleading

)eclare their organisation's interest so it is plain what and who is
being represented

- Declare in the IPR's Register the names of any public office-holders employed or retained by their organisation. Anyone can inspect this register
- Respect the codes of other professions and all statutory and regulatory codes in different sectors of PR practice, and warn their employer or clients about them
- Keep confidences, even after the connection with client or employer has ended, unless a court of law directs otherwise
- Not propose or take part in any action that would be an improper influence on public office-holders or the media. Some payments, gifts and inducements are, however, allowable
- Represent conflicting interests; competing interests, on the other hand, may be represented by agreement
- Not guarantee results when this is impossible. PR campaigns usually depend on factors which cannot be directly controlled by practitioners
- Register any lobbying interests.

The wording of the professional charter of the Public Relations Consultants Association (PRCA) is very close to that of the IPR's code. Both the International Public Relations Association (IPRA) and CERP, the European PR body, subscribe to a code of ethics which, if anything, has even wider implications. This expressly stresses the need to uphold human dignity, to contribute to moral and cultural conditions in which human beings can reach 'their full stature', and to respect the moral principles and rules of the Universal Declaration of Human Rights.

The law

Everything in the IPR code of professional conduct is subject to the laws of England. Obviously the day-to-day activities of PR people must be subject to the general laws of their country and more specifically to those that apply to their current sectors of work; thus, for instance, you must have a knowledge of company law, local government, general statutory controls, the law on charities, finance, health and medicine, race relations or equal opportunities. You need a passing acquaintance with several aspects of the law which touch on all public relations work and, increasingly, with European Union law. You need to be familiar with the law of contract so that you can protect yourself and your organisation from financial damage or unwanted responsibilities. The common-sense rule is to take all contracts with suppliers seriously, read them carefully word by word, and understand them. Unscrupulous lawyers have been known to change a phrase in a standard contract so that it seems the same, but isn't. The 'small print' on terms and conditions of business can be lethal for its omissions as well as being difficult to read.

A simple exchange of letters is usually all that is needed but when a supplier sends standard terms and conditions, read them. With photographic libraries, for instance, you will find costly penalties for loss of transparencies. Be sure to read quotations and estimates closely. Some printers will omit the cost of paper; designers tend to work in stages, so you need to be clear what you are agreeing for each stage. In offering public relations services always separate the fee element from the direct costs (all expenses raised in carrying out the work), otherwise you may find your client expects you to pay for them. It is standard practice for direct costs to be separate because you cannot be sure what they will be.

The copyright laws were extended by the 1988 Act. Your employer owns the copyright of any work you may do for them; but if you are self-employed, you own it (as first author), not those who commissioned you. Copyright can be assigned or transferred. You cannot, strictly speaking, unilaterally make changes to the work while the artist or author has the copyright. It is assumed that a photograph can be used for the purposes for which it was commissioned but if other opportunities arise the photographer has the right to charge a further fee. If you want the exclusive licence to use a photograph you need to have an agreement in writing. This still does not bring you the copyright. For that you should pay a fee and have a written assignment signed by the photographer. Most good trading relationships are not affected by such legal apprehensions, but remember both that disputes can arise suddenly through misunderstandings and that what isn't said can be as important as what is.

There is no copyright on an idea, only on its tangible expression. Verbal presentations, for instance, are not covered. So don't give away a good idea unintentionally. The 1988 Act introduced the idea of the originator having moral rights to be identified as the author and to be able to object to derogatory treatment of the work. This right is not automatic; it has to be asserted.

Defamation is another area of the law that can trip you up. Take care in speeches to avoid slandering anyone or libelling them in written material such as press releases or feature articles. The Trade Descriptions Act 1968 forbids false or misleading descriptions of goods or services. The IPR publishes a useful guideline to public relations and the law. These days, with more and more people ready to go to court, and the EU changing the ground rules, it is wise to consult a lawyer if you are in any doubt.

3

—— PRACTICE: PR —— AND MANAGEMENT

3.1   What management expects from PR

The nature of an organisation and its work defines its public relations activities. The extent of those activities and how they are organised internally and externally depends on economic conditions, the internal attitude to public relations, and management practice at the time. Recession and poor profits performance causes big companies to cut jobs. If at the same time there is technological change going on, making a cull of middle management easier, then you have the mid-1990s position of companies falling back on what they call their core business. This means far smaller PR departments than in the boom years of the 1980s and greater use of outside consultants for projects. In early 1994 the construction company Mowlem, in financial difficulties, simply axed its corporate public relations department.

In the very smallest organisations the chief executive is responsible for all functions; public relations, whether recognised as such or not, is one of them. In the activities of the chief executive are the embryo departments of the future. Going out selling: the sales and marketing department; dinner with the local MP: government relations; telling a journalist about a new product: press relations; helping a local school: community relations; telling the one or two staff what is happening and listening to their ideas: internal relations. As an organisation grows the most likely in-house development is to employ someone who can deal with advertising, direct mail, press cuttings and all the activities the chief executive regards as being part of promoting the organisation. This tends to put the incipient public relations functions under the umbrella of marketing. Media relations at this stage – for a company anyway – is more about product promotion than corporate reputation. If, on the other hand, the organisation prefers to use outside help immediately – thus keeping some of the activities separate – the public relations functions are less likely to be subsumed within sales and marketing.

The 1993 Stirling University survey of what organisations in Scotland expected from their in-house PR departments and from consultancies showed the top five needs as the same but considerable variations in importance for other functions. A media relations service was the most needed and, linked to that, formulating campaign messages. These purchasers included charities and National Health Service organisations as well as companies. From their consultancies they wanted advice on key issues, the organisation of functions and special events, and corporate PR services next.

EXPECTATIONS OF CONSULTANCY SERVICES	EXPECTATIONS OF IN-HOUSE DEPARTMENT SERVICES
1 Media relations	1 Media relations
2 Formulating campaign messages	2 Formulating campaign messages
3 Advice on key issues	3 Functions/special events
4 Functions/special events	4 Corporate PR
5 Corporate PR	5 Advice on key issues
6 Problem definition	6 Employee communication
7 Audience determination	7 Advice on public affairs
8 Advice on public affairs	8 Crisis management
9 Crisis management	9 Input on wider business decisions
10 Lobbying	10 Problem definition
11 Financial PR	11 Audience determination
12 Input into wider business issues	12 Exhibitions
13 Design services	13 Sponsorship
14 Employee relations	14 Design services
15 Issues management counselling	15 International
16 Sponsorship	16 Lobbying
17 Exhibitions	17 Financial PR
18 International	18 Issues management counselling

For in-house departments it was the same except advice on key issues came fifth, not third – a slight indication that management did not let the in-house departments take the part in policy making that it expected of consultancies. This reading is supported by problem definition and audience determination coming sixth and seventh respectively for consultancies, tenth and eleventh for in-house.

Advice on public affairs and on crisis management came half way in the priorities of both groups. Employee relations were seen much more as an in-house prerogative, but lobbying and financial PR were more likely to be sought from consultancies.

The two lists give a clear indication of the functions looked for today and the likelihood of them being organised in-house or through a consultancy. Fairly clearly then, advice on lobbying and financial PR would usually be bought in; sponsorship and exhibition work would usually be done in-house.

Design services would probably be bought elsewhere than either in-house or a PR consultancy. Research services, although not mentioned, would similarly be sought from different outside specialists (although often through a PR consultancy).

The functions tend to group themselves naturally:

1   Corporate relations, public affairs, issues management, lobbying and government relations, relations with pressure groups, sponsorship, community relations, international, crisis management

2   Financial and investor relations

3   Employee relations

4   Media relations, special events and functions, exhibitions.

The smaller the organisation, the more functions will be shared between a few people. The larger the organisation, the more they will become the responsibility of different people or different departments. The core business strategy, however, inhibits empire building. When consultants are taken on it is often for projects and not in a continuous fee relationship. A large business might once have had a manager for market research, another for internal relations, for public relations, for public affairs, for investor relations. Specific functions like video making, photography, print, exhibitions and conferences might have been handled internally too by different people. A period of cut-backs has a devastating effect on the assumptions behind such internal organisation. If you don't go into exhibitions any longer you don't need an exhibition manager. If you have less reason to make films and videos, that department will close down (like Shell's after 60 years).

People who used to do the work may team together to form a company and put in a tender. Some civil service work has been put out to what they term 'market testing', in a typically introverted way of looking at a trading function the wrong way round. They will test the market to see if the task could be accomplished successfully by outside companies or consultants, while themselves putting together teams to bid for the work. Local government, a sector in transition from doer to enabler, is also in a state of organisational flux.

3.2 Corporate communications

Public relations protects and projects corporate reputation, and helps create a trading environment in which the company can prosper. Its job is to provide information both to employees and to outside publics, and to ensure that communication procedures work well throughout the company. At the top level, public relations advises and counsels senior management, tries to anticipate the response of a company's various publics to management's actions, and helps manage public issues which affect the company so that the company's voice is heard.

It takes years to build a reputation; seconds to destroy it. The most famous example of this is now the Gerald Ratner jokes about his jewellery company's products being 'crap' and not lasting as long as 'a prawn sandwich'. The shares dropped from £4 to 7p.

There was a triple lesson here. His speech to the Institute of Directors in April 1991 had been checked by fellow directors – except he introduced the wisecracks afterwards. And he'd told the jokes before and they had been reported in the press. Things don't always go the same as last time . . .

In most plcs the head of corporate public relations (or affairs or communication) will be in daily contact with the chairman, whether over share price, suspected take-over, government relations, employee communication or one of the many issues – social, environmental, political or traditional – which affect operations.

The corporate public affairs function is a central one, working from head office and looking after the reputation of the company as a whole.

Because the activities of subsidiary companies affect the well-being of everyone in the group, the corporate PR unit must be able to influence the communications of operating subsidiaries. It will give advice, supply assistance, ensure that the graphic identity is imposed correctly, make sure the subsidiaries know the group's corporate objectives, and be around to help handle a crisis. In the international arena corporate PR will link closely with the operating subsidiaries and joint ventures, especially over social and trading issues, and relationships with official bodies. It will monitor the world and pick out issues that affect the group (if a subsidiary has not yelled first).

A corporate communications department

Taylor Woodrow is a UK-based group involved internationally in property, housebuilding, construction and trading. The group corporate communications department, led by Mike Beard, reports to the chairman on group matters, with a strong line to the group chief executive on operational support activities.

In the early 1990s it reduced in size to comprise a small, highly-qualified and experienced team of public relations specialists who work for about two-thirds of their time on corporate PR and the rest on operational support. The department recommends strategies and tactics to the group management concerning the company's reputation and positioning with key corporate publics. This includes programmes in financial communication and investor relations, public affairs, issues management, internal communication and contact with business opinion formers. The team's capabilities include media relations, advertising, print design and production, audio-visual, periodical production, the report and accounts, corporate identity, speeches and presentations, sponsorship and events management, display and promotional merchandise and *pro bono* projects. The team selects the most appropriate techniques according to the objectives of each programme and provides advice and support to operating management in all business areas as appropriate.

A team member is assigned to each of Taylor Woodrow's four business areas to act as a single point of contact 'account manager' when required. No attempt is made to carry out all public relations and publicity activities at the centre. Instead the team encourages each business to develop its own communications capability through a combination of in-house practitioners and external suppliers.

A communications manual provides advice and ideas to operational companies as well as defining the areas of activity where group coordination is considered to be essential. Apart from managing a wide range of public relations activities proactively, the department is the first point of contact for many external and internal enquiries about Taylor Wood-row. In a typical year it may respond to as many as 3000 media calls and 5000 general enquiries about the company.

PERSONAL DIARY

A day in the life of a corporate communications manager – Mike Beard, Taylor Woodrow

Work begins at around 5.20am. I set off with Colin Parsons, the group chairman, to the BBC Television Centre for his pre-Budget interview with Paul Burdon on Business Break-fast. On the way we discuss the likely questions and the possible effects of the Chancellor's Budget on our business. As usual the BBC has called us much earlier than we are really needed (so there's time to review current priorities while we wait).

After the interview we go on to the group's worldwide conference for 50 top managers. A leadership workshop is led by Will Carling, fresh from his triumph as captain of the England rugby team which had just beaten New Zealand.

There are useful exchanges among our team of managers from diverse businesses as they are updated on the group's strategy. During the afternoon session the corporate communications team is monitoring the Chancellor's speech, clarifying apparent anomalies and testing reactions.

At 5.30pm we brief the chairman for his follow-up interviews the next morning on Business Breakfast again and on the BBC Radio 4 Today programme. Then I leave for a charity dinner in London at which we have some good friends and contacts as guests. On the way I check with the department and find that all incoming calls seeking reaction to the Budget have been dealt with. I take their advice to make a call to the *Financial Times* to reinforce the response already given.

Just time to change for dinner. Have opportunities to exchange reminiscences and ideas for the future with good friends in the industry while helping a good cause. The event ends at about midnight. Not the end of a typical day in corporate communications – because there's really no such thing.

. . . and what one of his staff does
Karen O'Smotherly graduated from West Herts College with a diploma in international public relations and joined Taylor Woodrow's corporate communications department.
First function of the day is to scan the national newspapers for articles of interest for our business areas. I then read the day's press cuttings, Hansard extracts and attend to the first post of the day, addressing any urgent issues immediately.

My day is then a mixed bag of immediate issues. One is responding to corporate identity queries because we are a year into a standardised identity programme. Another is dealing with media enquiries about Taylor Woodrow Property Company as they come in.

My work has several constant elements. I write news articles for our in-house magazine. I am responsible for the design and production of any corporate literature or video. I may be called upon to help arrange a special PR function or event, often organising the media coverage as well. I work on the group public affairs programme, monitoring parliamentary and EU legislation and debate, as well as the political world. And there always seems to be a special one-off PR project.

So I am constantly juggling about ten issues or projects at any one time and must be able to switch rapidly between them. That variety means that every day is different and that's what is so challenging and enjoyable.

Mission and values

Since companies started to be called corporations (a useful, if portentous, term since 'company communications' lacks the grandeur of 'corporate communications') ways of expressing their personality and cultures have been sought. Small companies rarely write their aims down (entrepreneurial management may have changed course by the time the ink is dry). Corporations, on the other hand, usually have a 'mission', or more exactly, a sense of mission. Underpinning the mission statement will be a set of 'values'. Parallel with these will be a corporate identity. ('Graphic identity' or 'graphic style' are more pertinent terms for the logo or symbol an organisation chooses to represent itself, but high-flown phrases usually win these days.) It would, however, be better to keep the term corporate identity for the whole behaviour-style of the business: its culture.

The long chain of a company's desires begins with its purpose. Why is it in business? To satisfy whom? Some companies aim to satisfy their shareholders, the people and institutions that have bought a financial holding. Others look wider than that, to all stakeholders. These include the shareholders but also customers, suppliers, employees and the local community. Still others go further and treat the environment itself as a stakeholder. The more ethical and principled the purpose the easier it usually is to transfer a sense of mission to the employees.

To achieve its purpose, every company needs a strategy, a statement of where it aims to be commercially (in psychobabble, where it is coming from and going to), the position it wants in the market, the means it will employ, its distinctiveness. Plans are made by management to achieve that, to get from A to B. Tactics are the more detailed manoeuvres it will make on the way.

Values are the corporate beliefs of the company, its ethical stance, what it holds true, and stays true to. Strategy and values together will determine how a company behaves, what actions it takes, who it supports. Purpose, strategy, values and standards of behaviour combine to form a sense of mission. Mission combines a corporation's strategy with its culture (the way 'people like us' behave). Its values are settled in its culture. The difference between mission and vision is confusing. Mission is a timeless cause and purpose the company has; vision is the most recent way the company looks to the future. Vision is also more personal, more the current CEO's (chief executive officer's) sense of direction and current sets of goals for the company.

When a company's values are the same as its employees' values, and the values of the different departments (which may contrast strongly – just think of legal, accounts and public relations), its sense of mission will be stronger. That means that its public relations will be so much easier to coordinate.

Ashridge College's book *A Sense of Mission* suggests that strategy and shared values combine to create policies and behaviour standards as they affect staff, technical systems, skills, business style and organisational structure. The authors give examples of this for two different types of company.

SHAREHOLDER COMPANY	HIGHER PRINCIPLED COMPANY
Purpose	
The shareholder is king. Think of the pensioner living off investments	Be respected by our customers, our people and society
Values	
Individual responsibility. Autonomy and accountability. Efficiency is good. Victorian work ethic	Good people need space. Informality is good. Creativity is a human being's ultimate purpose. Caring is good. Borrowing is weak
Strategy	
Better financial discipline. Knowledge of cash cows. Skill at buying and breaking up poor-performing groups. Better operators	Better people, better motivated. Engineering excellence. New product development. Best after-sales service
Behaviour	
Budgets must be met. Managers work hard. Keep business simple. Decentralise. Focus on short-term financial performance	Management by objectives. Management by walking about. Open door. Team work. Communication. No borrowing

From a company's purpose, from its strategy, from its mission, the long-term messages that express its nature can be formulated. There will be plenty of short-term, tactical messages too, but it is repeating and adjusting the long-term messages that makes a company's corporate identity, in the broadest sense, recognisable, understandable and acceptable to its publics. In this context, the way messages are communicated has equal importance with content. 'Actions speak louder than words' is the cliché and the key. You can only make people aware of your intentions by telling them what you stand for. They need proof, and actions – behaviour – constitute that proof, that assurance.

Messages encapsulated in catchy slogans only bear fruit if they are demonstrated in everything the company does. Vacuous sales claims, superlatives in press releases, the leading-edge, bigger-better-quality-service semantics of immodest hucksters are best avoided.

The channels of communication should suit the message, and feedback by surveys, if affordable, are important. Such an approach may signal the need for changes in the company's policies, reveal actions and messages that are implicit within what the company has done but which have not been drawn to the attention of its publics. Many companies behave well but do not think to talk about it. One of the most important functions of corporate public relations is to tease out the hidden good news and pass it on. Messages should, where possible, be tailored individually to the different publics, remembering that people 'buy' what interests them. Some will welcome profits, others want evidence of service to the community. Above all, be honest and do your best to avoid the suppression of anything the public has every right to know.

Issues and public affairs

If public relations is to have true status within a company it must examine the business plan in the context of trading, political, economic, technological and social trends. From this analysis it will be able to assess the wisdom of the board's intended actions. Business people can be blinded by what they want to achieve to the foolhardiness of trying for it when conditions are wrong, support is weak or the outside world likely to be hostile. Paradoxically, of course, that is exactly what true entrepreneurs do (when everyone else thinks they shouldn't) – their will-power, dominance and gut feel sees them through. The secret is usually in the degree of exposure and the size of the company. No news may be good news.

It is in the handling of issues that public relations becomes public affairs – concerned with the impact on its business strategy of social and political change outside its control (but possibly within its spheres of influence). Issues can range from the social acceptability of products to possible changes in the law or company policy on the disabled, the environment or charities. If a company is to influence the course an issue takes it will need support. That support will only be the more forthcoming if the perception of the company by potential supporters is accurate and favourable.

Herein lies one of the more glib, but nevertheless cogent, arguments about public relations. In the world of the mind there are no absolute truths ('there is nothing either good or bad but thinking makes it so' – *Hamlet*). Consequently perceptions are all, and they need to be nursed or corrected. No one sees everything; we all see in our own glimpses, remember only part of what we see (and usually what someone else would rather we didn't). In public relations, perceptions have to be taken as fact. Research is irritating when it shows what people think and you know that to be erroneous. It's no use going along with management in saying, 'Rubbish! That's not true! We'll ignore it.' What people think, rightly or wrongly, must be treated as fact – it's a fact they think that, whether its true or not. They must be persuaded otherwise (or the company should realise they have a point, and adapt).

Management must determine which trends are an issue for the company in case they damage or even destroy it. Professor Tim Traverse-Healy suggests eight criteria:

1   Could the issue affect the company's bottom line?

2   Is the 'bad news' scenario realistic?

3   Could corporate action halt/amend/modify/delay the progress of the issue?

4   Will our present policies and practices stand up to public examination?

5   Are the resources to act available?

6   Is the cost to the company acceptable?

7   Is the will to act present?

8   What would be the effect of inaction?

'Only when the range of issues has been considered,' he says, 'can those few that are likely to affect the achievement of the bottom line targets be isolated. Only then can the decision-making models be drawn and the specific role-players, junior and senior, be nominated. Simultaneously, the company's position has to be set out, debated internally, and agreed.'

Twenty per cent of IPR members, many of them working in corporate communications departments, say they have lobbying responsibilities. Even the arcane complexities of policy-making can be affected by an organised approach, if you start early enough.

• Find out. Collect information on the issue and the organisations concerned

- State the problem and the ideal solution
- Identify the publics – the ministries, the officials, government agencies, relevant organisations and supporters
- Write a précis strategy saying what needs to be done. Pay particular attention to timing in relation to the political process: green papers, white papers, Select Committee stages
- Approach the specific publics – legislators, civil servants and others you need to convince – with your case. Depending on the issues this could involve meetings, visits, seminars, media relations
- Steadily work at contacts in the corridors of power so that there is a groundswell of awareness and support
- Apply pressure through knowledge of how the various institutions work. This is the time for parliamentary questions, for the support of MPs who agree with your case, for responsible and informed media comment
- Monitor progress in all corridors of power, including the media
- Adjust your strategy in the light of feedback. You may realise you have to settle for less than you set out to achieve
- Don't stop – keep the relationships you have forged going, ready for next time. Personal links are valued highly in this sector. Having a reputation for providing sound information, and having antennae for political situations is a worthwhile lobbying weapon in itself.

The five most important pieces of advice are: to start as early as possible; to find out as much as possible; to pick your targets and communicate appropriately with them; to keep your messages short and the pressure on.

CASE STUDY

Changing the law

In the summer of 1988, 17-year-old Kate Stone lost her life in a car accident. The car in which she was travelling was driven by a 17-year-old learner driver under the supervision of a 17-year-old friend of Kate. No other cars were involved. Kate's mother, Vicki, set out to change the law. She began with:

- a petition
- correspondence
- local police support
- support from local groups.

Next she canvassed leading insurance companies and road

---

safety bodies. Legal and General asked their PR consultants, Dewe Rogerson, to help Vicki. They drew up a campaign strategy:

- establish clear objectives
- have Vicki as the campaign spokesperson
- raise public awareness through the media
- enlist support from influential third parties
- encourage the public to raise the issue with MPs
- persuade the Government to amend the law to have, first, a higher minimum age requirement than 17 and, second, that minimum to be 21 with three years' driving experience.

No UK or EC statistics were available. The target publics were the public, third party bodies, the press, and policy makers and opinion formers. A Private Member's Bill was considered, but rejected in favour of obtaining an amendment to regulations. The following were arranged:

- A PO Box was set up as a central point of contact with the public
- The Learn + Live identity, based on the L plate, was created with the subtitle: Parents' campaign for safe driving tuition.
- Campaign launch at the House of Lords
- Motoring organisations approached for support
- Briefing note to MPs interested in road safety issues
- A meeting between the Minister for Roads and Traffic and Mrs Stone
- Press conference with the Minister and Mrs Stone, announcing proposals for minimum age and experience conditions.

In 1990 the law was changed: to give instruction to other drivers you have to be at least 21-years-old and to have been a qualified driver for three years.

UK political background

Knowledge of the way political institutions work is essential. The House of Commons Public Information Office (set up only in 1978) is your first resource. It publishes (on subscription) a weekly bulletin, fact sheets (which demystify political jargon) and offers a telephone enquiry service. It subscribes to POLIS, the Parliamentary On-line Information System, and using this can yield considerable detail. Bills, Acts and many more interesting publications are available from Her Majesty's Stationery Office in London. Daily proceedings for both Houses are available. A pleasant way of keeping up with politics when you want to be aware, is to subscribe to *The House Magazine*. If you are more seriously involved you will probably decide to subscribe to a monitoring service. That way you will be able to keep track of Hansard, debates, motions, statements and answers, Select Committee meetings and standing committees, amendments to Bills, Early Day Motions, HMSO documents, parliamentary procedure, information on MPs and Peers, and ministerial statements.

You can arrange a similar service for the EU to cover annexe debates and proceedings, legislation, resolutions and written answers, Commission proposals, Court of Justice cases, committee membership and details of MEPs. Parallel information is available for lobbyists in the United States of America.

The most obvious contacts if you become concerned with lobbying are your own member of parliament or member of the European parliament. MPs and MEPs like clear, concise, preferably one-page briefs (imagine how many are sent). They will sometimes attend well-organised meetings on industry topics and visit company premises. But don't expect them to come: the information you want to give has to be useful to them. (Regional statistics, for instance, could be used in a debate.) Find out if they are likely to be interested first, by consulting political directories like DODS or Vacher's, or monitoring parliamentary questions they ask. The party conference or half-yearly meeting can be a sensible time to liaise with individual MPs and meet other people with political interest or clout.

Other, often neglected, potential allies can be opposition party MPs, political advisers within ministers' offices, party research departments, independent political bodies (like the Centre for Policy Studies), pressure groups (they welcome natural allies), and Whitehall civil servants who brief EU counterparts.

Two important organisations to know about – and both run informative conferences – are the Industry and Parliament Trust and the Whitehall and Industry Group. They help MPs and civil servants understand industry through a shadow system. However, many MPs and civil servants believe it is even more important that industry leaders come to understand the processes of government for their own good. If you want to develop your knowledge of government, begin by reading *Parliament: a brief guide*, written by Dermot Englefield for the Industry and Parliament Trust.

Your simplest guide to the civil service is the Cabinet Office publication, *Finding your way round Whitehall and beyond*, by David Laughrin. Influencing Whitehall successfully early on can save frantic struggles later, although it is a matter of pin-pointing the right people (who may be involved in early drafting and may not be top civil servants at all), and being well-informed and open. Compared with the more cooperative EU staff, Whitehall has had a reputation for inaccessibility. The signs are that this is changing and the new 'business' ethos engendered in civil servants, coupled with helpfulness being one aim of the Citizen's Charter for public services, should speed it along.

The Government Information Services do not claim to do public relations as such, seeing themselves as passing on information rather than actively persuading. But the range of technical services they provide government departments, agencies and public sector clients is central to communication. The route to media contacts within government is the 'white book' guide to *Information and Press Officers in Government Departments and Public Corporations*. It used to be free to journalists and PR people but now you have to pay for it.

PERSONAL DIARY

A week in politics
In 1987 Mark Oaten was in the first group of thirteen students for the West Herts (then Watford) College diploma in international public relations. He is now a director of Westminster Communications, the government affairs specialists.

I knew that an Account Executive had nothing to do with ledger books but remember being disappointed that my initial training placement was with Shandwick, a company I had never heard of. They employed me after the course and I spent the first six months exploring where I would be best placed in their empire. I settled on Shandwick Public Affairs where, as a local borough councillor, I developed a portfolio of local government clients. Three years later I moved on to become account manager at Westminster Communications. My attempt to get into the other Westminster failed at the General Election. After a year I was made a director.

I have a particularly important reason for being thankful for the course – it was there that I met my wife, Belinda.

This is a week's diary as it came off my computer:

Monday
Meeting – the Audit Commission
Meeting – Laser FM radio station.
Notes: Do marketing proposals, brief designer on logo, draft housing conference speech.

Tuesday
Commission Management meeting
PR Department meeting
To Oxford – Vale of White Horse Council
Canvass for local elections.
Notes: Draft media plan for local government restructure, brief TV training people, send photos to the Commission, new business plan.

Wednesday
Meeting – Sir Keith Speed MP
Lunch at Rodins with *Accountacy Age*
Harrow Council meeting with Housing Department
Watford Borough Council meeting.
Notes: Read 'Well Children' report, fix Radio 5 meeting, finish design work, speak to *PR Week* about survey.

Thursday
Westminster Communications board meeting
Meeting – design consultants
Meeting – designer of Castle Point logo
Meeting – District Audit Services
Meeting – Liberal Democrat HQ at Cowley Street

Friday
Meeting – Castle Point planning
Final planning meeting – local elections in St Albans.

The European Union

One way to ensure that Britain will be a successful country is for its industry to look for opportunities in Europe, for the country to accept the European idea and become first-rate at negotiating beneficial economic and political conditions. In Europe, with institutions being reshaped, new relationships forged, new patterns of influence arising, Britain will have to play a full part. Sound knowledge of the EU is therefore also a current affairs essential subject for anyone in public relations.

Lobbyist Douglas Smith sees the EU as a more refreshing, fluid market place for ideas and power-broking than Westminster and Whitehall. The civil servants hunt for information and pass it around. Press, television and radio coverage has probably more significance because of the need for good domestic coverage. The media in Brussels is also close to the detail of what is happening (and there is no Official Secrets Act so information for briefing documents is more available if you look). Organisations need a lobbying arm that is on the spot.

Des Wilson, an advocate in the court of public opinion, as he terms himself, offers these guidelines in the handling of public affairs:
- Tell the truth. Professionals worth their pay are not in the business of telling people what they want to hear
- Find the common ground. Eliminate those areas caused by misunderstanding
- Respond positively, openly. If you treat pressure groups, the public or concerned citizens with arrogance, you make them angry
- Break down the stereotypes. If you have a case, argue it; don't just attack the messenger. If you pigeonhole an organisation you may fail to assess its strength accurately
- Assume responsibilities that are yours. The best public relations is to do what's right
- Address the issue directly, at source. Life is a trade-off but you've got to be willing to trade.

Financial public relations

Financial public relations is the broad umbrella term for all financially-related company contact within corporate communications. Of all PR sectors this is probably the one needing the most specialist knowledge. More than average numeracy is helpful but not essential. More important is an insight into investment, a convincing grasp of the sequences and timings of the different financial procedures, an up-to-date knowledge of the rules that apply in financial relations in different countries, the requirements of stock exchanges, and familiarity with financial analysts, the financial press, radio and television programmes and their needs.

The starting point is the regulatory framework of financial communications. *The Yellow Book* lays down the obligations of listed companies; the *Rules of the Panel on Takeovers and Mergers* details conduct on those activities; the Companies Acts are specific on disclosure in the annual report and new requirements for corporate governance have been laid down. The Stock Exchange publishes *The Regulatory News Service* procedural guidelines.

These on their own give you fundamental information but no sense of direction. Nor are they an easy read. If you work in financial PR, either inside a public company or with a consultancy, you will need to take especial note of the rules about insider dealing, because you will often have information that others do not. European law has made controls more stringent.

CASE STUDY

A corporate centenary

The centenary of a telecommunications company that needed to establish a much higher public profile than in the past, at a time when it was going through extensive change in ownership, structure, manufacturing methods and product range. It had a long-standing reputation and many innovations to its credit. Planning began seven years ahead. The elements in the programme were:

- A travelling roadshow lecture
- A special exhibition in the Design Museum, London, with a royal opening, and a 25-minute film shown there continually
- A company history was written and published, and the IT minister launched it; given to employees, pensioners, customers
- Much educational material for schools: wallcharts, video, teachers' notes and pack, brochure for secondary schools
- A series of events at different company sites included: celebration at a local castle; a Centenary cake; go-kart races; fireworks; open days; an operetta; sponsored runs; parachute drop for charity; lecture by a science celebrity; schools competitions; parties for pensioners.

Consequences

The effects of the programme were to make the company much better known at an important time in its business history and to demonstrate its professionalism. Its reputation as a 'thinking' company grew because it tried to explain the implications of technology rather than concentrate only on its products. Timing was good as a preparation to creating a new corporate identity shortly afterwards. The general public came to hear about the company in a significant way and there was excellent feedback from government, customers, schools, local communities, pensioners and employees. Related to the budget the programme gave value for money.

PR advice to other corporate centenarians

- Don't be self indulgent: history alone is insufficient reason for a celebration
- Think carefully how to use the past to position your company for the future
- Plan with care
- Think carefully about both internal and external publics
- Be original.

(The above is the structure of the centenary of Standard Telephones and Cables in 1983.)

3.3 Internal relations

If it is not careful, public relations will lose its fight for a say in the handling of internal communications. Present players in the field include human resources and personnel, sales and marketing, IT, public relations and communication management specialists. They need to get together. The Industrial Society, long-time proponents of team briefing and cascade systems, say that it does not matter where the responsibility for internal communications lies as long as there is one. More important than specific methods of internal communication, the Industrial Society believes, is 'the organisation's whole attitude to its employees and its willingness genuinely to share information and take time to listen to its employees' views with respect.'

As things stand there is no hard financial evidence that companies which stay hierarchical and simply tell employees what to do (who then do it from 9 till 5, go home and get on with something else) are not successful businesses. Smaller companies are more likely to be able to operate this way than large ones because the lines of command are short. The larger and more dispersed companies are the harder it is for everyone to know what's going on.

Even the judgement of excellence at a particular time is no guarantee of continuing business success. Witness the troubles of some of the well-known and much praised companies described in Tom Peters and Robert Waterman's book *In search of excellence* published in 1983. The Industrial Society conducted a survey in January 1994 of how 915 companies communicated internally. Noticeboards were used by nearly everyone. Close behind (82%) were team briefings.

The survey was biased in two respects. First, most respondents were in human resources and personnel. So it is not surprising that the returned questionnaires (from 3584 sent out) showed that specialists involved in employee communication reported to personnel or human resources departments (62%). The other definable reporting centres were: the chief executive officer (15%) (more likely on small sites), corporate communications (8%), and marketing (2%). On large sites 30% reported to PR or corporate communications.

Secondly, all respondents were taken from the Industrial Society's own data base. This suggests that they were already more than averagely interested in employee communications, and team briefing in particular. A second survey, of all those who did not answer the first questionnaire, would be useful to test whether they did not reply because their internal communications were embarrassingly primitive or because they were too busy to bother. That notwithstanding, the survey draws a pertinent picture of employee communications in the mid-1990s. Nearly three-quarters of companies had no written policy and only a third linked internal communications policy to the strategic business plan: two failings that public relations should rectify.

The time spent on internal communication was rarely costed and three-quarters allowed no specific budget. The one in ten that did costings averaged £290 for each employee each year and mainly accounted for spending on print (62%). Other costs stated by these 90-odd respondents were employee surveys (38%), employee events (36%), and videos (36%).

The most common ways of communicating to employees were: noticeboards and team briefings, newsletters (78%), house journals (65%) and roadshow meetings (53%). E-mail (38%) was more frequently mentioned than video (29%). For feedback from employees the main two methods were 'walking the job' (70%) and team briefings (65%). Consultative councils or committees (49%), quality teams (47%)

PRACTICE: PR AND MANAGEMENT

and meetings with the unions (44%) came next – although, as the single most effective means, meeting union representatives was only 4% compared with feedback from team briefing (24%) and walking the job (26%). Other channels used were suggestion schemes (36%), big meetings with employers (24%), focus groups (22%) and speak-up systems (10%).

Some of the tools

- *Team briefings* The cascade idea of team briefing is for directors to brief top management, top management to brief middle management, middle management to brief supervisors and work group leaders, who brief their teams. Meetings should be short (say half-an-hour), face-to-face, in small groups and allow for responses. They should be held regularly, perhaps once a month, and set up well beforehand, preferably at a constant date and time. Ideally, anyone briefing a team will have their immediate boss present. Content is usually a 'core brief' which will be consistent throughout the cascade, general information about the local unit, information specific to each work group or team. Performance measures for the team will normally be included. Videos can be a useful aid.

  Communication training for work leaders is essential. The problem with people is that they don't always come up to idealised textbook prototypes. 'Those who communicate are those who lead' is all very well but only patchily true.

  Many good communicators are, as the old saying has it, empty vessels (making the most noise). Many people who are brilliant at their jobs and who lead by example, find communication unnatural. The weak links in the team briefing cascade system are the length of the chain and the quality of the personal communication.

- *Key communicators* Many extensive PR campaigns needing to communicate information internally use a system of key communicators. This to some extent gets round the standard team briefing weaknesses by additionally using people with good communication skills to provide a second, more personal, injection of information, discussion and feedback.

- *Management sessions* Some company CEOs hold occasional informal meetings with different groups of senior and junior managers. Senior managers visit sites where they have no line responsibility, attend team briefings, walking the job and answering questions.

- *Speak-up systems* These allow employees to say what they think without fear of being victimised for speaking out. Either employees are able to by-pass their own manager (who will not be told) or to ask questions anonymously for them to be answered in the company newsletter or E-mail system.

- *Tapes* Some companies build up a stock of videos which can be borrowed. Others will make one main video a year to convey the annual results. Companies with a high proportion of sales representatives will often make audio-cassettes to take advantage of the time they spend in their cars. High-cost communication has to be queried when a company is doing badly.

What to communicate

The Confederation of British Industry offers a check list:
- *Progress*: product sales; market shares; financial results; contracts; circulation figures; accident record; export sales; company achievements; competitors' products; new products; departmental performance
- *Profitability*: the basis of costs/prices; need for profit as a return on investment for shareholders and for reinvestment in the business
- *Plans and policies*: take-overs or mergers; supervisor development; job evaluation; reduction in staff; expansion plans; board-level decisions; factory reorganisation; a new consultant; the pension scheme; employee financial interests and saving schemes; car purchase; pay bargaining rules
- *People*: appointments; resignations; labour turnover; promotions; overtime/short-time; internal vacancies; grievance procedure; training courses; staff handbook; absenteeism; job security.

Quality matters will be high on the agenda and so should be recognition of people's achievements. In true two-way communication there should be no difficulty as team members will say what they want to hear about. Remember that all internal communications go outside the company when the employees go home. Messages that will cause dissension or that will feed competitors valuable information (even of morale) must be carefully thought out.

The advance of high-tech

Internal communication will be affected by the new technologies every bit as much as external communication. Not long ago computers were main frames, typewriters were manual then electric, duplicating machines used waxed stencils for press releases, messages went overseas by telex. The most salient comment on the D-Day commemorative activities in June 1994 was that the massive organisational achievement of the landing in Europe was accomplished 'in a world without computers'.

Now communication is digital and technologies are converging so that one piece of equipment can perform several functions. (A mobile phone, for example, can also fax and send an E-mail message to someone's personal computer.) Computers can take dictation, being able to react to your voice (and even italicise if you say 'italics' and 'end italics'). PC screens are being made interactive, so those who suffer from technophobia need not use a keyboard.

In 1994, the communication management consultancy Smythe Dorward Lambert, wanting to find out how high-tech was likely to change internal communications up to the millennium, surveyed 83 companies and IT specialists. Nearly half thought that high-tech was already having a serious impact. They divided digital communication into two: voice and data, and face-to-screen technologies. The first group includes facsimile transmissions, E-mail, voice mail and personal organisers. Very few companies in the survey did not use fax. E-mail was rapidly on the increase. Both these were used to pass operational information to staff.

Telephone conferences were used regularly by half the companies, voice mail less so but it was also on the increase both for sending instructions and passing business information to managers. Face-to-screen systems include video (used by half the companies for getting across important business messages), video conferencing, and business television. Video conferencing saves on travel and can be used for both managerial and operational information exchange.

In big companies, especially those with many sites (dealerships for instance), business TV is already becoming an expected part of reinforcing the company culture and keeping everyone up to date. Some car manufacturers regularly send out live programmes on satellite link-ups. BMW beam half-hour programmes twice a week. Pearl Insurance have piggy-backed on BMW's network. Ford show programmes to assembly line staff. One development could be for hotel groups to set up business TV units so that dealers can go along to a local hotel to obtain their timed culture-fix over satellite.

What effects will these developments have on internal communication? Smythe Dorward Lambert predict a change of role for middle management as more messages go direct. Senior management will be able to communicate directly through E-mail to everyone with access to a personal computer, and talk to all employees through business TV. Without intermediaries, messages may well be clearer and senior management will become better known to employees. Equally, the need for senior management to acquire televisual skills will become more pressing. Meanwhile, face-to-face contact could diminish.

In companies like banks, with many points of contact with the general public, the manager will diminish in power and the front line staff, with their computers, grow more important. The CEO and senior management could be acting more in a support capacity for front-line staff, thus turning the traditional management pyramid on its head. As Anthony Greenwood of Smythe Dorward Lambert puts it: in the 1980s the customer knew best; in the late 1990s customers will know more. This effect will be global, for both internal and external communication. Through multi-nationals and companies networking around the world, information will become widespread, passed on electronically in seconds. The shortage of Inkata stickers in the South African election of May 1994 was first picked up by an Internet subscriber in London, from the voting bulletins appearing in the network.

At the same time, the growth of external electronic link-ups, and in particular Internet with its global chit-chat, makes it harder and harder for anything in the electronic networks to be kept secret. Hackers will exist in many companies who can break into the secure files of management or staff. Goodness knows where all this information may end up. Some will regularly be leaked to the newspapers by E-mail; they, in turn, will be enthusiastic Internet users. Round and round we go. Team briefing could become more important for explanations and understanding than for passing information (much of which may be known already). Team briefing takes time; E-mail takes a second or two, across continents.

Electronic networks are breaking down already fragile barriers between internal and external communication. This means that companies, especially those with many overseas partners, will have to plan extremely carefully and quickly how they release information, or they will find it is known already. Whose message is it anyway? What can we stop them from knowing rather than what do we want them to know?

Instant communication runs the risk of separating bald facts from understanding. Therefore it becomes important to manage the many different options for communicating through different channels, and for reinforcing messages. Use of inappropriate channels could invest a message with a significance it doesn't have. Once when staff were called together suddenly in the canteen it presaged take-over or liquidation. Now it is likely to be only the latest live on-air TV programme from the company broadcasting studio with the CEO being grilled by a professional presenter.

Best practice

The Centre for Communication Development, a Smythe Dorward Lambert offshoot, suggests a model for internal communication best practice, see Fig. 3.1.

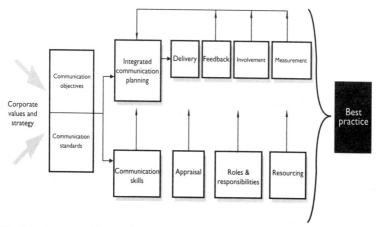

Fig. 3.1 Elements of best practice (Courtesy: Smythe Dorward Lambert)

Best practice has these ten aims:

1 To have clear objectives for internal communication that support the business's objectives

2 To develop standards for internal communication which also help measure performance

3 To create an annual communication strategy by matching internal communication with the annual business planning processes, having a system that picks out the information needed, and a way of reviewing issues on which the business will take a position (both internally and externally)

4 Communicate by knowing the information needs of the different internal publics, having one system which transmits urgent information quickly and another which provides structured, face-to-face meetings in a style matching corporate values. Back this up through consistent, appropriate print and electronic media directed at the different internal publics

5 Encourage employees to have a regular say by building in ways

they can express their views. Feedback mechanisms should be regular and understood by management and staff

6   Involve employees in issues which affect them before decisions are made

7   Give communication skills training to help selected groups of employees communicate better. Link this to the human resources and personnel appraisal system so that competencies are recognised

8   Measure the effectiveness of internal communication and review methods regularly to improve performance

9   Define and publish people's roles in communication at all levels of the organisation

10 Provide proper management and financial resources so that the objectives can be achieved.

THE HAWTHORNE STUDIES

A study on lighting in work areas in 1925 showed that workers responded with increased productivity to both better and worse lighting, and that even where the light stayed the same there was improvement. The researchers concluded that people were working harder because they were being studied. This became known as the Hawthorne effect: the tendency for research subjects to change their behaviour in reaction to special attention. (The research was at the Western Electric Hawthorne plant in Illinois, USA.)

When three years later interviews were arranged for workers to air their feelings about their jobs and company, they often said it made them feel better about things. A final study of a bank in 1931 suggested that the productivity level was related to the social pressure of their colleagues to comply with group norms.

These studies meant that communication was not just a hierarchical series of orders but had strong social connotations:
- Human communication had a strong influence on a group's behaviour
- Feedback from workers could be useful
- Informal channels of communication exist that management is not aware of.

THE TWO THEORIES OF WORK

Theory X
People dislike work, therefore need to be controlled, do not want responsibility but only security.

Theory Y
People will work hard if they want to get satisfaction, can direct themselves when committed, will take responsibility under the right conditions, can be creative at work and are, in fact, an under-used resource.

CASE STUDY

Internal communications

Two major sites were to close and 5000 employees to be made redundant in the Military Aircraft Division of British Aerospace early in 1991. An employee attitude survey showed that managers were secretive, the company had to change to survive, and employees needed to know much more about performance and plans.

The internal communications department, under Maria Gill, was part of the human resources function. The main elements in the plan devised by internal communications were:

1 *Draw up a formal communication plan*   Publish this and use the presentation of it as an example for other top management presentations

2 *Plan redundancies and site closures carefully*   Break the news, explain the reasons, limit demotivation, use comprehensive support material, talk to the local community, provide counselling for employees

3 *A series of seminars for the top 500 managers*   To promote the necessity for change and gain their commitment

4 *Cascade the results of the seminars*   To all employees, using extensive support material

5 *Line managers to deliver important messages*   To use the team talk procedure, business plan briefings, cascade

messages, hosted lunches, discussion forums, listening groups, walking the job

6 *Tell everyone the business plan every year* Give each of the 20,000 employees a copy at special briefings

7 *Improve team talks and encourage feedback*

8 *Use electronic media* Sending fax messages by computer to six sites cut the time for receipt of an urgent message from a day to 20 minutes

9 *Encourage upward communication* Through listening (focus) groups on business issues, the team talk procedure, senior management walkabouts, involvement-based suggestion schemes, quality improvement groups, random sampling, opinion surveys, cross-functional project teams, feedback questionnaires, letters pages in newsletters and journals, manager-hosted lunches

10 *Publications should support business objectives* A single magazine replaced several publications, site newsletters addressed local concerns

11 *Different themes every month* Different themes chosen each month for all communications media, from publications to team talk, informal briefings and walkabouts

12 *Spread knowledge of best practice* Using IT message distribution and work groups

13 *Involve families* A new publication for employees' families, open days, employee visits to other sites, community activities (soccer schools, photographic competition), improve communication locally

14 *Measure change by employee attitude surveys.*

Two years later Military Aircraft's managing director Kevin Smith said they needed 'to bring the same level of marketing and strategic thinking to internal communications as we apply when we are chasing a major sale. The transformation of our business prospects over the past two years has been due in large part to getting people focused on our business objectives. And that in turn has to be largely due to the clarity and drive of our internal communication.'

4

—— KNOWLEDGE: ——
FIELDS OF STUDY

4.1 What you need to know

Study the syllabus for a university public relations course to understand the combination of background knowledge and practical skills thought necessary for a competent graduate in the discipline. Most of today's practitioners do not have this knowledge; increasingly, tomorrow's will.

When you start in PR, you will not use much of this knowledge. If you are good at writing, that's what you will do most; if you are good at organising you will find yourself running events; if you have specific knowledge of an industry sector, that will probably come in more useful than your theoretical knowledge of, say, how government works or the different theories of communication. You may not know too much but, as in any walk of life, if you are personable, impenetrable, sharp-witted, selfish and good at delegation people may not catch on to your lack of knowledge until you have plugged the gaps, by which time it won't matter. You get other people to do the work, reporting to you, while you look after the client, the overall picture, yourself. Students on placements tend to notice these things. One, reporting on his experience at a consultancy, wrote: 'There are two types of people that remain at the agency – those that have few options, and the good looking people who enjoy having their egos massaged. The former are expected to undertake 75 per cent of the workload, and be happy, while the latter spend most of their time being carried by the former.' An example of the Pareto principle at work in staff employment.

Students from Bournemouth University, reporting back on their 1993 placements, were asked to say which parts of their studies they found useful (or not) and what they would like added. This is what five of the students said:

Working in a management consultancy

Most useful: electronic publishing and computer skills, and writing skills. *Occasional use*: law, organisational behaviour, public affairs, finance and accounts. *Add*: better grounding in printing processes, presentation skills, photography.

Working in a charity

Most useful: media news values, theory of communication strategies, writing skills. *Occasional use*: knowledge of attitudes, behaviour and influences as an analytical tool. The course builds self-discipline and develops time-management skills. *Add*: a working knowledge of the many photographic and broadcast media formats to avoid being over-charged, fooled into accepting avoidable delays and poor quality repro-duction.

Working in a leading consultancy

Most useful: writing skills, public affairs, media training. *Less useful*: organisational behaviour (difficult to apply). *Add*: media training, media production, more practical writing practice (charity press kit say), study of voluntary sector (many students obtain early experience in this field), more emphasis on current affairs.

Working in a medium-sized consultancy

Most useful: the general foundation of knowledge. *Add*: photography, design, media training for interviews and announcements, more time for writing skills, more case studies.

Working in a local council

Most useful: writing skills. *Occasional use*: general knowledge of public relations, marketing, opinion assessment, campaign evaluation. *Not specifically useful*: finance and accounts, law. *Add*: photography, design.

Obviously, the nature of public relations work varies according to the organisation it is for and the level at which it is being carried out. The universities monitor the balance between academic, technical and professional studies through feedback from their students (Bourne-mouth University adjusted their course to take their students' experi-ences into account).

The four-year BA (Hons) Public Relations course at Bournemouth has three components which are considered fundamental: professional PR theories and skills; business and management; communication pro-cesses. The first two years give a broad foundation. Placements are organised for the third year. In the final year students proceed to 'professional skills and strategic insights integrated into public relations as the management of corporate reputation'. They each take on a research project. They each study one of three sectors of public relations practice: PR for marketing, corporate PR or European PR.

The first two are seen as 'pathways that mirror the major divide in professional practice as support for marketing and as public affairs'. The third is offered because Bournemouth thinks Europe will grow in professional importance. Even if most of its graduates do not work in Europe (the university offers language options) they will deal with Europe. This divide shows the complications of learning public relations. It is an indication that you only know what you practise. But, as one student on placement reported: 'Much of what was learnt in the first two years has become so ingrained in my knowledge databanks, the skills have become so much second nature, that it is difficult to identify them as skills learnt at university.' (A few years ago he would have said 'memory' for 'knowledge databanks'.)

The first level of this course, then, deals with introductory theory and practice of PR, the general political and economic background against which it works, contemporary media and society – because 'much of the work of public relations practitioners takes place within the world of the media' – marketing, written and visual communication ('persuasive writing and good visual communication are core skills for the public relations practitioner'), learning a language, the option of studying inter-personal and group communication, and computing and data manipulation skills.

The personal communication option teaches social skills, communication in and between small groups, handling conflict with other people, negotiating, interviewing methods, coping with stress, planning public presentations and handling the media. The computing module is based on the assumption that 'public relations employers now assume that you can word process, operate simple databases, do basic document designs and produce graphics'.

On the second level of the course (their second year) students learn how to plan public relations campaigns, develop their political, economic and governmental knowledge (the external influences on organisations), understand how attitudes change, and improve the range of their writing and presentation styles. They will know the basics of commercial and media law as they affect public relations practice, especially confidentiality, negligence in consultancy, copyright, defamation, corporate law, contract and consumer protection.

PR practitioners need to know how businesses are run, how they work from a financial perspective. Time is spent therefore on understanding balance sheets, the profit and loss account and cash flow, on the use of financial ratios, on working capital, assets, gearing and return on equity, on the presentation of accounts, European accounting practice, and who the financial publics are.

Finally, they have the study of behaviour and communication within organisations as an option. The object of learning about theoretical sources and models for business organisation and organisational communication is so that they can analyse and interpret behaviour at work. Once again the students could well join companies that employ PR staff who know far less about the subject than they do. Students will know about group behaviour and leadership, strategies, management styles, motivation, power and cultures. They will have studied the management of change and creativity. They will have practised techniques like team building, group decision-making, group and individual appraisal and assessment systems. So they should not feel out of place in organisations that are themselves only just discovering them. Young people with this background are likely to be more flexible than established staff because they have not had time to be threatened by change and the idea of change is part of their stock-in-trade from the beginning.

After two work experience placements in the third year, the students' fourth year is spent on a research project, studying issues management and corporate reputation, and one of the three career pathways offered (PR for marketing, corporate PR or European PR).

Research

By carrying out a research project the students kill three birds with one stone: they study an aspect of public relations, they practise research in a formal framework, and they produce a comprehensive written report. Many of these studies, from Bournemouth and elsewhere, are already adding to the complement of knowledge available to the PR profession.

Research reports by the first graduates of Bournemouth's PR course ranged from the role of PR campaigns in the repatriation of Vietnamese refugees from Hong Kong and issues management in cities' tenders for the Olympic Games, to the effectiveness of shock tactics in charity appeals and an evaluation of PR in the social services. Students sometimes found that theory and practice were at odds: 'Life Office PR Operations Follow No One Pattern of PR Theory' was the title of one dissertation.

Research plays an increasing part in public relations thinking and the students have to know the fundamentals. In a research workshop they learn the approach expected in carrying out their projects: defining the methodological problems or issues, forming a hypothesis, working out their research plan (qualitative and quantitative methods, population, sampling, questionnaire design, how to conduct interviews), how to approach field work, to code and analyse results and present the findings.

Their projects thereafter have seven stages: defining the subject for research and the fields of observation; conducting literature surveys and using appropriate research methods; collecting evidence and data and testing their validity; framing hypotheses and drawing conclusions.

Issues management and corporate reputation

Studying the political, economic and governmental environments in which organisations operate is of prime value in issues management. The problems of specific industries (nuclear, oil, chemical, food and so on) march with the issues of the times (environmentalism, consumerism, privatisation, European integration . . .) and the preoccupations of pressure groups (such as, say, animal rights) to create both threats and opportunities.

This is the high ground of public relations, helping to manage issues in an organisation's operating environment, contributing to power relationships as well as communication. Issues affect organisations' reputations – a 'phenomenon central to public relations' say Bournemouth. Their method of study is by analysis of case studies, so that students learn to evaluate first the potential of a range of issues and then the public relations strategies, reactive or proactive, for dealing with them.

Public relations for marketing

This is an area responsible for so much contention between PR and marketing people (which is part of which, which is more important?). Those who believe in all-embracing public relations will tend to choose public affairs. Those who want a more immediate living will lean to marketing support. Those who feel European can become experts in the complexities which will govern our futures – and hope to reap the rewards of specialist knowledge in an expanding field.

Study is broken down into consumer PR, business-to-business PR (one company trading with another) and advertising (recognising 'the strategic and tactical interdependence of advertising and public relations in campaign planning').

The consumer module teaches branding, purchasing behaviour, the product life cycle, market segmentation, choosing PR techniques in relation to marketing strategies, and how a company's aims mesh with those of its marketing and PR. It includes public relations activities specific to the consumer market: giving advice, making presentations, briefing the media, understanding news and features, running a press office, print, audio-visuals, competitions, events and customer care programmes.

Communication with opinion leaders is included because their activities affect sales of consumer products and services, and with trade bodies because of likely common interests. In any case, communicating with opinion leaders is a prime function of all public relations management. Crisis and issues management, and lobbying, come into the picture through product withdrawal decisions, health and safety arguments, and the need to defend positions affected by the law and pressure group influence.

The business-to-business module covers industrial products, high-tech, professional services and the voluntary sector. The advertising module brings knowledge of how advertising agencies and design studios work, the links between PR, advertising, marketing and communication, briefing suppliers like designers and photographers, and an appreciation of the advantages and disadvantages of advertising.

Corporate public relations

The practice of public affairs demarcates public relations from marketing support and, says Bournemouth, 'represents a distinct, exclusive field for professional growth'. At the end of the module students should be able to contribute to lobbying, supplier relations, sponsorship, corporate identity campaigns and community relations.

The City of London is where the money is. While it is harder for most students of public relations to find jobs in financial PR, once they get established the sector pays well. It is here too that public relations consultants have fought to be on a par with bankers, accountants, stockbrokers and lawyers in being able to charge in relation to results. With the fortunes at stake in takeovers, privatisations, mergers and flotations, being part of this action is worth the effort of acquiring the specialised knowledge needed.

The second module in the Bournemouth corporate public relations course covers investor relations. Here all the normal principles of practice apply but in relation to very specific financial publics – the various stakeholders with an interest in a company. The emphasis is on the needs of companies quoted on the Stock Exchange to raise finance and see that their share price is fairly valued.

Study necessarily and vitally includes the regulatory framework, financial system and calendar within which investor relations operates. This is constantly changing and the practitioner in this area has to be bang up to date. This, indeed, is part of the allure of financial and investor relations – it and public affairs have a ring of importance that is missing from the more directly sales-orientated sectors of PR. Secondly, knowledge of the many special situations common to the City is needed: of a flotation, a rights issue, loan raising, takeovers and mergers, share price defence and international listing. Thirdly, continuous study of the current economic background is essential, of what affects markets, globalisation, Eastern Europe, the prospects of a single European currency and the possibility of Frankfurt replacing London as the main European financial centre.

Strangely, more than a good GCSE level grasp on numeracy is not essential, although a head for figures helps. Many is the merchant banker who could not do algebra. Judgement, familiarity with the markets, the different industrial sectors covered in the business pages every day and, above all, an up-to-date knowledge of both financial and communication procedures in set situations. These are the skills needed above and beyond those of sound public relations practice. Just as lawyers find a niche in public affairs, so stockbrokers find one in financial communications. They add communication skills to their special knowledge. It is harder for you to add their kind of knowledge to public relations skills.

The final part of this university course on corporate public relations is devoted to strategic management and organisation. The knowledge imparted can hardly be used by anyone starting out in PR but is of considerable relevance to young managers. Public relations is nowadays contributing to corporate strategy in a way rare even twenty years ago. Chairmen who believe their company's strategy is right are concerned that it can be ruined by poor communication. That opens the door to public relations influences on strategy; certainly on planning. To enjoy this you need to be of a managerial slant of mind. Much of the study is heavy going. But it is here that the strength of public relations will be and where, if you hope to land heavyweight jobs in PR, especially inside companies, you need to direct yourself.

Bournemouth's course begins with an introduction to the nature of corporate strategy, the strategic management process and the contribution of public relations; with strategic analysis, choice and implementation, strategic decision-making in practice (case histories), problem awareness and solution development, culture and (again) strategy. This is all followed by strategic analysis, strategic choice and strategy implementation. Without going into detail, some of the skills acquired are: analysing the corporate environment, analysing resources (value chain analysis, experience curves), power and conflict (groups, coalitions, stakeholders); evaluation and choice, differentiation, analysing returns (profitability, cost-benefits), risk and feasibility, selecting strategies; allocating resources, organisational structures (functional, holding, matrix, hybrid), human resources, people and information systems, cultural change, managing the change process.

Europe

The third option is European Public Relations. Bournemouth is very optimistic about this because it has been given added force with the closer ties of the European Union. UK business must look after itself against a more integrated Europe and public relations departments need 'a detailed knowledge of the different social, political and economic conditions in each country, and an understanding of their implications for communicating with strategic publics'. The first part of this option includes the growth of public relations in other European countries, knowledge of European media and media politics, comparative methodology for international social research, European PR case studies, and trends. The second part looks at the functioning of multinational companies in Europe, the community institutions and law making.

4.2 Psychology and public relations

'Of course public relations is about psychology. It's listening to the other fellow's point of view and trying to persuade him of your own.' This was written in one of the first issues of the IPR's journal *Public*

Relations, about half way through this century. Persuading someone to your way of thinking is not just a mental exercise. It is done for the most part to alter attitudes and to try to influence behaviour that stems from another way of thinking.

Changes in attitude do not necessarily lead to changes in behaviour. There are other factors: the social norms of what may be acceptable and the will, the intent to change behaviour. In public relations terms, changing the behaviour of identifiable groups of people (publics) is the objective. It may be over voting, or buying non-leaded petrol, or not buying fur coats (or making them); acting more tolerantly, giving equal opportunities, stopping swearing, buying one product rather than another, wearing seat belts, shunning racism, using s/he instead of he. Building a relationship is one way of bringing about behaviour change (come on, support us). Boards of directors want their publics to back their companies' commercial objectives. They want to minimise opposition, win understanding, keep things as they are. The price of this influence may be an equal and opposite flow of information from publics to company that changes the company's behaviour. Feedback from its employees, from the local community, from pressure groups, may persuade the company to change its way of doing things – to communicate better, pay more, cause less social nuisance, support the nearby community, change its approach to the environment. Threats, implicit or otherwise, and changes in the law, are also effective ways of changing behaviour – without bothering with building up a relationship.

Good public relations practice is closely dependent on good psychology. Involvement with the behaviour of people and groups in a social setting is involvement with social psychology, which studies behaviour, how people think and feel and behave in society.

Psychology is the study of mental and emotional life, of what goes on in people's minds. Knowing that is a problem in everyday living, for how can you get inside someone else's mind to find out? Barry Unsworth made the point in a lecture on truth and lies in fiction, that you learn more about people's thoughts and feelings from reading about imaginary characters, than you do in real life. Similarly, Peter Middleton, chief executive of Lloyd's, told an IPR City & Financial Group meeting that he had given up reading books on management, preferring poetry and novels because they help you understand people.

If what goes on in people's minds influences their behaviour, as it must, and public relations is closely concerned with behaviour, and psychology is the study of behaviour, then PR is applied psychology. This is the argument put forward by Dr Jon White of City University Business School. He sees the main threads of psychological thought as part of the body of knowledge which should inform public relations practice. But he also believes that most practitioners are unfamiliar with basic knowledge of psychology as a separate area of study. Dr White sees psychology applying to public relations in three broad areas:

- as an aid to planning programmes, carrying them out and evaluating them
- in the relationship between the client and PR consultant: defining the problem, negotiating and giving a good service
- how PR practitioners do their jobs.

Over the last century psychology has evolved through a number of schools of thought. Here, briefly, are some of the main themes.

Psychophysics

This is the study of human sensory capabilities, the work done by our eyes, nose, ears, taste buds and skin. Studies in this aspect of psychology began in the 1870s with the work of a German philosopher and first experimental psychologist, Wilhelm Wundt, in setting up psychological laboratories to study sensations.

Techniques used in the study of sensation are extended to bodily changes, to learn about emotional states (blood pressure increasing for blushing, for instance; the saliva glands being inhibited by fear so that your mouth goes dry; or glands opening so that you sweat profusely). This led to the modern development of the polygraph or lie detector. In everyday relationships a recognition of the body's chemistry and emotional signals can influence your behaviour towards someone. In crisis planning, PR people who are relatively cool headed and physically unaffected by pressure are going to be good members of a team.

Functionalism

At the turn of the century another school of psychology asked not 'what is consciousness?' but 'what is it for?' Much of their work was on the learning process and, as such, links to behaviour. The most famous example is Dr Pavlov's conditioned response experiments with dogs. By serving them food just after a bell rang he found that eventually they salivated at the sound of the bell.

People's learning processes are of singular interest in public relations work. Can a response be predicted if a certain stimulus is given? Providing a reply-paid card triggers more responses than just leaving it to the recipient to write in or ring up.

Gestalt psychology

Around the time of the First World War, another German psychologist, Wolfgang Kohler, made experiments that suggested that insight and the whole pattern (in German: Gestalt) of an experience is more important in giving it meaning than its parts. For instance, a caricature of someone in just a few lines conjures up the whole of the physiognomy. Separate dots in a cross formation are interpreted not as separate dots but as a straight line. Optical illusions, as in the work of Escher, further show how the brain makes assumptions from its previous experience and for a time does not know what it perceives.

A simple example of this effect in PR terms is in personal presentation: certain signals sent out – a smart suit, polished shoes, and expensive watch – suggest a certain type of person. Which may not be true. Often it isn't, certainly not when solicitors have their untidy, threatening clients dress smartly for trial. Perceptions may be dictated by patterns in the mind. Do not make assumptions.

Psycho-analysis

This is where Freud comes in. Psycho-analysis is the study of the inner workings of the mind. Freud posited the existence of the unconscious mind as a trigger for behaviour that cannot be explained by the rational appearance of things. An analyst works a 'cure' by guiding conversations with a patient to draw experiences out of the subsconscious so that they can be recognised and dealt with. The work of the psycho-analytical school included Jung (the desire to belong) and Adler (motivation is driven not by sex but by the desire for mastery).

The ideas are relevant to public relations in its links with human resource departments and the use of personal profile tests. Jung's extrovert–introvert distinction, and its extension into the 16-type Myers–Briggs interpretation of people's personalities, can be used in recruitment and team-choosing.

Much work in advertising, brand and corporate image is concerned with the unconscious, with beliefs just below the surface. Advertisements are part of contemporary mythology, the themes that run through written material: good, evil, dirt, cleanliness and so on. They resonate with people's collective beliefs. One example Dr George Gaskell, a social psychologist of the London School of Economics, gives is the purity of white cleansing materials (soaps, powders) against the 'blackness' of bacteria: 'There is almost the idea of separating the clothes from the dirt that has penetrated them. Tide's in, dirt's out.'

A couple scantily dressed, bodies entwined, eating ice cream. We are not shown fat people, unpleasant skins. The ad identifies with gratification. Here's something that young, slim, attractive people can take part in. A virtue is created out of the associations. As people assemble consumer products around them they are assembling identities (even though in reality there may be very little difference between the products behind the brands). The brand images allow us to buy into a particular lifestyle. This is the world of semiotics and Benneton advertising, of projective techniques, focus groups.

Behaviourism

Judge people by their actions, not by what they say they will do: actions speak louder than words. If there were no distinctions between how you say you will vote and how you act at the moment of voting, we would only need a statistically flawless sample and you needn't vote at all. Behaviourism is associated with the American psychologist John Watson. It emerged just before the First World War from experiments on animals which concentrated only on their behaviour in response to stimuli. Soon studies of human behaviour were made. One suggestion was that if you can control the environment in which people live and work, you can control their behaviour. Prison is one example. Putting humps (the old 'sleeping policemen') down on roads makes drivers reduce speed or go along a route the planners prefer to be used. The law is probably the most successful way of changing behaviour (of law-abiding citizens anyway). Would most people have worn seat belts or limited their drinking if no penalties followed?

A strong back-up element in both campaigns, however, is the attitude of one's peers. There is risk of social ostracism if you do not change your behaviour to conform with that of people you socialise and work with. Examples abound in the 1990s: smoking, drink-driving, racism, being culturally insensitive, chauvinism, stereotyping and so on.

Self-regulation is a peer pressure way to avoid unwanted laws being brought in. This is a continuing debate so far as lobbyists are concerned: should there be a register, should lobbyists be regulated, should parliament do it or the lobbyists themselves, or their professional bodies?

The behaviour of groups is of especial concern in public relations. The more information that can be obtained, the better a public relations campaign can be planned. Know thine enemy, so to speak.

Social interaction

A school of psychology grew up in the 1930s which argued that we learn about ourselves from our interaction with others. This is the theory of the looking-glass self. Each person is a mirror in which we are reflected and see ourselves. At the individual level an example of this is frequent in relationship counselling, where one partner is annoyed by the behaviour of the other. The realisation that this behaviour is itself caused by reaction to the behaviour of the partner who is annoyed, can bring about some seeing of ourselves as others see us. The behaviour of groups (publics) can be similar.

Cognitive psychology

Cognitive means knowledge of. Cognition means your thoughts, knowledge, interpretations, beliefs, understanding and ideas. Cognitive processes are your mental processes of perception, memory, the way you process information, make plans and solve problems. Cognitive psychology is not concerned solely with the human thought process but has been extended to such modern studies as artificial intelligence – trying to make computers think. When you join or work for an organisation you have to get to know it, the way it thinks and behaves corporately, its culture and practices, its mission, motivations and values. This is the world of corporate public relations and internal relations.

Cognitive dissonance is one of the psychological phenomena best known in public relations. Consonance is when feelings or attitudes are in harmony in a person; dissonance is when they fight each other, and cause discomfort. The theory is that people's attitudes are usually consistent with each other (consonant), so that they will tend to shy away from conflicting ideas. If, as so often with today's change management culture, you are forced to change your attitude, adopt a new procedure, then cognitive dissonance occurs. If you believe a supplier is giving you good service and you trust him, you experience cognitive dissonance if you are forced to obtain three quotations and to choose the lowest.

Smokers who believe that smoking is harmful may look for evidence that it isn't, so that they feel more at one with themselves. Predicting behaviour is harder with people who are in a state of cognitive dissonance (when, say, their religion cuts across their liberal beliefs) than with those who have strong, consistent attitudes.

Cognitive psychology gives rise to what is now called *the theory of reasoned action*. It suggests that our behaviour is influenced not by what people will really think about us over an action, but by what we think they will think. Behaviour can be changed it says by such approaches as offering new beliefs or getting rid of old ones, by weakening or strengthening confidence in existing beliefs, by altering the relative importance of people's values, or by changing the balance of opinion formers that influence your behaviour.

Social psychology

Here psychology is concerned with behaviour in social settings, with attitudes, prejudice, group behaviour, social interaction. As such it holds supreme interest for public relations practitioners. Public relations is concerned with changing both attitudes and behaviour. These are essential areas of study in social psychology.

Sometimes attitudes are deep-seated, stemming from our upbringing: you 'learn' to have a successful attitude in a particular social context, and it is reinforced by approval. If you want to be part of a particular social group you usually have to adopt or naturally have their attitudes. You also develop attitudes out of personal experience: you talk critically of a product that gave you trouble. When others suffer similarly, like say railway passengers, you get together and form a pressure group because you want to change the railway's attitudes and behaviour. They in turn want to change the group's – by winning more understanding of the problems or improving the service.

Attitude change

Changing attitudes – the structures in the mind – is not easy. There is low correlation between what people say they will do and how they behave. Attitudes have three components: what you know or believe about something (cognition); your emotional response, how you feel about it (evaluation); and your verbal or behavioural responses (behaviour).

The psychologist Fishbein argued in the 1960s that attitudes are formed from people's individual salient beliefs, those things that spring to mind when you think about an issue or topic. These will be about seven in number (plus or minus two), the normal extent of short-term memory.

Each belief is for or against the topic and, therefore, evaluative. General beliefs, however, do not predict specific behaviour (being religious does not determine your views on having women priests).

When asked questions most people won't say 'I don't know', yet very often they have little knowledge of the subject. Very often in opinion surveys people will, in Dr Gaskell's phrase, 'create a response on-line, picking up the most available and accessible piece of information, even from within the survey itself'; from a news bulletin, a conversation, the response alternatives in the survey.

For example one of the questions in the Ofwat survey on water regulation was: 'Are you satisfied with the safety of your tap water?' The average person has little idea about questions of water quality or safety. These attitudinal responses are likely to be highly unreliable. The context set by the questions may well be suggesting what an appropriate answer might be.

Attitudes guide information search: people are more inclined to read about things with which they agree, but in the political domain are more even-handed. MORI have shown that party-political broadcasts are watched by people with a reasonable cross-section of political beliefs. Attitudes are part of the judgemental process of how we decide about things. The halo effect is that when you generally think good things about a person you tend to support whatever they do. Typical is the bias of the football supporter.

The theory of planned action suggests that we do not choose to do things which we think are beyond our ability, no matter how attractive the result would be. Voting is easy but giving up smoking or going on a diet are hard. Our self-expectation is high in the first, low in the last two. This theory suggests that behaviour can be changed by reinforcing the belief that doing something will bring a particular result; by suggesting other ways of achieving the result; and by underlining and providing the skills and resources needed. Encouragement by getting you started along the path will be a good move – recipes for dieting and a system of rewards would be part of the campaign.

Attitudes control recall of information, what comes to mind on a subject, the agenda on a particular issue. Exposure tends to lead to positive attitudes, as with the idea of familiarity leading to favourability. The more frequently people see particular advertisements, the more favourably inclined they are likely to be: we go with what we know and are a little suspicious of the new. If two things are associated, one positive and one neutral, the neutral thing will tend to take on positive character-istics. This association of ideas is the basis of sponsorship.

Social learning theory examines how someone takes up the attitudes of another, as children with their parents, and with role models. McGuire posits five stages in changing attitude. The first two are to do with reception: get people's attention, reach the audience; and make sure they understand the message. Then they need to accept the con-clusion (yield rather than resist), remember the message and then act upon it. When studying groups under controlled (laboratory) conditions often as many as 30–40 per cent will change attitude along the lines one wants. In the real world (the field) getting an attitude change of 3–5 per cent would be excellent. The reason is to do with motivation which, in the laboratory, is high because of concentrated attention and the time that is devoted to the experiment.

Petty and Cacioppo proposed the elaboration–likelihood model. Some-times people will weigh up arguments logically, when they are inter-ested in an issue (the central route to forming an attitude). At other times they won't have a Fishbein balance sheet in their minds, will not give a matter much attention (the peripheral route), and will take short cuts, act on impulse, make superficial judgements.

The central route to persuasion is cognitive, logical and thoughtful. The *peripheral route* is superficial, more to do with the way the message is put across than with the meaning of the message. It is more a lure, but by the same token is transient and easily countered. The central route needs concentration, repetition, time, a clear message and to come via a written rather than an audio channel of communication. If these are not present persuasion will be better tried along the peripheral route. The central route depends on the strength of the message and how it is elaborated convincingly. The theory suggests that successful persuasion completes five stages: attention-getting, understanding, elaboration to convince, integration (agreement) and retention (making the new idea part of yourself).

Guy Fielding, a psychologist at Queen Margaret College, Edinburgh, suggests that public relations practitioners need ideally to persuade by the central route, and sees other communication industries – advertis-ing and design for example – as being more concerned with the periph-eral. As the targets of persuasion usually decide which route they will take, part of the art is to create and support conditions which encourage the central route to be chosen. If this is impossible, then start with the peripheral route with the intention of creating conditions where a central route campaign can be introduced.

The trouble today is that more and more people only seem to want to respond peripherally. There isn't the time for deep thought. Words are not meant to be read any more; they are merely part of designers' seductive patterns. The medium is the message after all. It was Marshall McLuhan who opened the way for impression marketing, that stimulator of the impulse buy that would reasonably be better left on the shelf.

Why are so many best sellers bought by people who don't read them? Why are so many Christmas presents never used? How can so much interest be whipped up for a transitory privatisation campaign? It's the success of the peripheral route with people who do not really want to pay attention, preferring to succumb to visual and affective blandishments. It's heartening that Guy Fielding identifies public relations with the central route.

Behaviour can change attitudes. The classic instance is the idea of smiling when talking on the telephone: an originally grim, early morning attitude can be converted to a pleasing telephone manner in moments.

Corporate image can be seen as a kind of gatekeeper or filter to attract people's attention. Changing attitudes is not easy but psychological research indicates strongly that it depends very much on the credibility of the communicators, on the prestige in which they are held, on their standing and lack of bias. Another factor is the nature of the communication method: does shock-horror work, or softly-softly? Also the role you are asked to adopt has a strong influence on your attitude to others. A role play of 'prison warders' and 'prisoners' quickly got out of hand.

Psychological studies that are especially important in today's society and today's organisation, are of prejudice, discrimination, stereotyping and conformity.

Diffusion of innovation

Fifty years ago researchers thought of the mass media as being a powerful and immediate way of sending messages direct to individuals. This one-step concept was compared to the effect of a hypodermic needle and was part of the stimulus–response (Pavlov) school of psychology prevalent at the time. American research in the mid-1950s however, suggested that a second step was involved in bringing about action: the effect of personal contacts and networks on the decision was recognised and thus opinion leaders (friends, colleagues, acquaintances whose opinion was valued, not necessarily public figures) conditioned responses to media messages. This led in turn to recognising the influence of interpersonal (social) relationships in decision-making and to the idea of diffusion of innovation as part of the process of intentional social change. This is the jargon term describing how new ideas (products, services, theories) come to be adopted by publics. The mass media inform you, but people you trust persuade you.

Whereas opinion formers (gatekeepers) and the people who follow them are usually very similar in views (part of the same social group), with the diffusion of innovation the influential groups tend to be different. This is because an idea takes time to be adopted throughout the community. The decision-making process is seen as passing through five stages: awareness of the new idea, persuasion (form an attitude to it), decision, use, adoption or rejection. People are grouped into five categories and the messages that are put out to persuade them may well be different. The innovators love something new; the early adopters are the opinion formers; the early majority follow their peers; the late majority are the sceptics, perhaps forced into choice through need or social pressure; the laggards are the traditionalists who look backwards not forwards. Study of the characteristics of each of these groups is worthwhile. One conclusion from the research was that discussion groups helped speed up acceptance by lowering the chances of individual thinking. People adopt because of relative advantage: the innovation is better. It must also fit in with people's values and not be too complex. Finally, if other people use it, that encourages change.

Diffusion theories

Groups of diners tip less than one person dining alone (because the sense of obligation is diffused). People pulling on a rope pull harder when doing it alone than when working in a team. The influence of the leader can be diffused. This has been given the name 'social loafing' and it is something to think about in the modern fashion for teams and teamwork. But if a task is made more challenging or the team see themselves as making a unique contribution, social loafing decreases.

The social impact of any source of influence on a target individual increases with the number, immediacy, and strength or importance of the sources.

Management is always in search of definites, assurances, guarantees. How can you manage if you cannot measure? (Quite easily, if you know your people and they are good. The problem seems to be finding the people – hence the stress on training, job evaluation and review.) There is a growing need to underpin PR service with research findings. The distinguished social psychologist Kurt Lewin holds: 'Nothing is so practical as a good theory.' In short, the use of psychology and communication theory research lend credibility to PR claims, just as the theories in management books underpin the credibility of management.

Obedience to authority

A book on the murder of Jews under the Third Reich concludes that most of the 'evil men' were just ordinary people following orders from superiors. An American experiment in 1963 showed that 65 per cent of volunteers for a 'memory test' gave a subject electric shocks and continued at high voltage levels when urged to do so, even though they disliked the procedure. (Luckily – but unknown to them – the subject was an actor and no shocks were transmitted.) What makes people conform to the system? How much unquestioning conformity is there in organisations today?

Influence by minorities

Persuasion by a minority – even of one (Henry Fonda in Twelve Just Men) – can change the attitude of the majority if the minority has a consistent position, is not seen as rigid, dogmatic or arrogant, and represents a developing social norm in society. Feminist and multicultural issues are examples.

Cognitive response

The cognitive response theory proposes:
- That if you read a communication you will tend to persuade yourself for or against the argument in accordance with the balance of arguments in the communication. Opinion change later correlates with your support for the arguments, with your recall of your reaction, but not with your recall of the arguments themselves.
- That a persuasive communication will be unsuccessful to the extent that its target can argue against it.

Presenting arguments

Should you give a one-sided argument or present both sides? Biased arguments reinforce prejudices. Presenting counter arguments weakens these. But if you are communicating with people who disagree with you, two-sided arguments are better. Being aware of opposing arguments makes one-sided communications less persuasive than a balanced view. A danger is that balance gives counter-arguments, and the refutations of them.

A strongly substantiated attack on a belief markedly diminishes your support for it. But a weak attack, subsequently refuted, means you are better able to reject a strong attack. You have been inoculated (McGuire, 1961/4). Forewarning of an attack gives people time to construct counter arguments. You become aware of manipulators' knowledge of this technique the more committees you attend.

Heuristic theory of persuasion

When people are heavily involved in an issue the more strong arguments, the better. But too many weak arguments are worse persuaders than a few because people generate more counter-arguments. If, on the other hand, people are not very involved in an issue, many arguments are more convincing than a few, regardless of how strong or weak they are.

Heuristics are a short-cut way of reasoning, deducing a probability rather than a certainty. 'Messages with many arguments are more likely to be effective than messages with few arguments' may be a general rule of thumb but it is unlikely to be true of people who are not very involved. Similarly with 'Arguments made by an expert are more valid than arguments made by an non-expert' (Petty, Cacioppo and Goldman, 1981).

Conformity

Even though the correct answer is obvious, if several people in a group collaborate to give the wrong answer, the odds are that an independent individual will agree a third of the time in a series of tests. Three-quarters of independent people will conform at least once. (What will they think of me? What will they think I think of them?)

Other research-based findings which may usefully be taken into account when planning public relations campaigns are:

Availability error

This is the tendency to make judgements on the basis of information that is readily available – or more noticeable or highly publicised or dramatic or pictorial – without finding out the full facts. A similar phenomenon is the halo effect whereby one feature, good or bad, dominates judgement unfairly.

Primacy error

This is the error of going on first impressions, an especial weakness of interview techniques. It includes a tendency to take notice of information given early rather than late. This underlines the importance of press releases and videos giving crucial information at the beginning.

Attenuated effect

We live, says McGuire, in an age of diminishing expectation. When social marketing started it was thought that big campaigns, like health, would have a substantial effect on the population. It turned out, however, that long-term changes in behaviour of only 5–8 per cent came about after years of effort and high expenditure. The message becomes thinly spread.

Distal measure

There is still a view that if something gets on television everyone will change their behaviour, but this is not the case. Exposure, indeed, is but the first of perhaps a dozen steps towards changing behaviour; it is away from the centre (distal).

Neglected mediator

In building up a campaign, something that has high impact, like humour say, may interfere with understanding: you remember the joke or the comedian but not the product, particularly if it is not well known. If you are trying to get over a new name, introducing music, songs, humour may have undesired effects.

The golden mean principle

Intermediate levels are generally preferred to extreme levels. It does not follow that, if a little fear moves some people to action, then a lot of fear will move everyone. Extremes will tend to be less effective.

Situation weighting principle

Where you already have a well-informed population, a low level of persuasion will work. If there is ignorance, you need to raise anxieties more. Any communication has to be set in the context of the level of concern and knowledge of the target audience.

Phenomenological studies

This is the approach to personality that tries to understand behaviour from the way individuals see and interpret events. Carl Rogers believed that people are motivated by the 'actualising tendency' to fulfil their potential and want to behave in ways that fit their image of themselves. They will tend not to deny themselves new experiences.

Abraham Maslow believed motivation stemmed from a hierarchy of needs. The needs at the earlier levels must be satisfied, at least in part, before the individual responds to more distant levels. The chain goes: food and drink; safety; belonging; gain recognition and esteem; knowledge and understanding; aesthetic needs; realise potential in self-actualisation. (Altruism and care for the greater welfare of society, the apparently natural progressions, are missing at the top of this pyramid.) Maslow studied leaders in different disciplines who had been remarkably successful at fulfilling their potential (self-actualisers). From these studies he decided that the following factors lead to fulfilment.

- Experience life as a child does: become absorbed and concentrate
- Don't stick to the tried and tested: do something new
- Do not be led by authority but by your own feelings
- Do not live life trickily but be honest
- Stand up for your own views even if they are unpopular
- Assume responsibility
- Work hard at everything
- Identify the barriers to your 'self' and bring them down.

This thinking is behind modern liberation movements, especially feminism.

5

SKILLS: WRITING, — PRESENTING AND — MEDIA TRAINING

5.1 Writing well

Writing changes with its format and vehicle: scribbled note, report, speech, press release, letter, advertisement, instruction leaflet, corporate brochure. Writing also changes as its purpose changes: to inform, alarm, persuade, dissuade, plead, record, impress. The words you choose, the punctuation, the length and complexity of sentences, the tense, mood, voice of verbs, all need to be appropriate to your audience. Writing shows what is in your brain, what you are thinking. 'How do I know what I think till I see what I write?' commented novelist E. M. Foster. Good writing is under threat; indeed writing is under threat. If you are disorganised mentally, your writing will betray that: you will repeat yourself, paragraph carelessly, verb badly (the Americans can make a verb out of any noun). If you use loose sentence constructions, wild adjectives, long words (to impress), you are telling your reader about your mental state. Worse, you may not get your message across. Clear writing is simply the logical use of words and punctuation to convey information and ideas.

Perhaps your PR career will not be in sectors where you need to write well. Or you may be adept at persuading (or instructing) others to write for you. Many high-flying PR people, like many senior managers, hardly put pen to paper, fingers to keys. All they have to do is give approval.

This is not necessarily a bad thing because it gives work to 'ghost' writers, personal assistants, secretaries, journalists, PR departments and consultancies. In business, content and action are more important than style. Writing rarely makes money but it should convey sense. If you are interested in writing well, consider first the modern threats to coherent, clear use of language:

1 *One of many PR tools* In public relations, writing is just one means to the end of running a successful campaign or programme. It is too often downgraded as merely a technical skill. Writing formulates ideas, is part and parcel of mission and value statements, written strategies, plans and proposals. But the ideas, timing and action in PR work come first. The object is to communicate an idea so that it will be accepted and acted on; good writing may be peripheral to that.

2 *'I was sick as a parrot, Brian'* The spoken English of popular broadcasting – whether Colemanballs commentators or soap opera informality – has become a strong influence on the use of language. Greater informality and acceptance of dialect at the cost of understanding do not necessarily communicate better. Expectations of the more formal written word become lower.

3 *One picture is worth . . .* Words are giving way to visual messages. It's an audio-visual world and multi-media disks are beginning to compete with books as educational tools. The linear way of learning, by reading sequences of words from left to right, will compete with the ability to select images in any order you like: hear a tune, read a few words labelling an image (there are writers who specialise in this), watch a video, click for more information.

Where words are used in highly-designed magazines, often magazines about typography, the text is used as part of the visual pattern rather than as something intended to be read.

4 *Incomprehensibility* Jargon provides short-cuts to communication between equals who know the meanings. Use jargon out of this context, to blind with science or just to sound self-important and knowledgeable, and understanding is lost.

Modern business has its own jargon: try 'empowerment', 'ownership', 'positioning', 'prioritise'. You will read many times about PR programmes that are 'thoroughly planned, strategically timed, carefully targeted and highly focused', about 'comprehensive public relations strategies'. Public relations people, anxious to impress, can write like this: 'The brief is multi-form, not only on an advisory level but also to conceptualise, contextualise and implement a working strategy . . . ' Or this: 'Well-researched communications messages, disseminated through appropriate influence channels to target professional audiences . . .'.

Here are more examples, from award-winning Sword of Excellence entries: 'watched a satellite downlink'; 'all spokespeople were media trained'; 'differentiate from the competition by positioning the consultancy as thought leaders in . . . '.

5 *Multi-cultural influences*   English, said Enoch Powell, is our language. But it isn't any more. Perhaps 350 million people speak English as their mother tongue, and they include English, Scots, Welsh, Irish, Americans, Canadians, Australians – all of whom give it their own quirks, spoken or written. Another billion people can speak or understand English. Perhaps two billion use it in some form, if you include pidgin versions. It is the language of business, of politics, of science. Multi-cultural, multi-ethnic influences are changing English, redefining what is acceptable, extending meanings. The overseas effect on English (as understood by people born and brought up in Britain) is to introduce a second vocabulary for use in business meetings with executives from different parts of the world. Non-native speakers of English give words different meanings which follow a kind of logic but are not Standard English.

Consider 'The lecturer gave the facts shortly, hardly presented his argument, and at last gave a prevision of the future of PR. He said that these days there was more competence.' Consult the glossary of Offshore English given by Vincent Guy and John Mattock in their book *The new international manager* for a translation: 'The lecturer gave the facts briefly, forcefully presented his argument, and, lastly, gave a forecast of the future of PR. He said that these days there was more competition.' Guy and Mattock remark that if your English is too good you won't be wanted at meetings attended by non-native speakers of the language.

6 *Ignorance rules OK*   It is harder nowadays to maintain what is good English and what is not. Dictionaries are circular in their definitions: they set out to record how words are used. If they are used incorrectly, that is how they are used, so the dictionary includes what were once incorrect meanings. Except how can you have a correct or incorrect meaning if words mean what you

say they mean? Imply, infer; refute, deny; anticipate, expect; aggravate – to make worse or to annoy. All the time this goes on, nuances of meaning are lost; sense becomes more difficult to follow. Misunderstandings abound. Perhaps they can be clarified when spoken; but you won't always have the author with you when you are trying to make sense of a document.

7 *Lowest common denominator* The Adult Literacy and Basic Skills Unit has estimated that 6.5 million Britons have trouble reading, writing, speaking or understanding English. What is to prevent their impaired ability setting the norm? If you wish to communicate with this 6.5 million you need to approach them in their terms. The written word may be useless.

Vocabulary moves towards the lowest common denominator. Good communicators rarely dare use words that would improve people's vocabularies (if the reader bothered to look them up). The risk is too great.

8 *Who knows?* If your bosses are not particularly literate, they will not know whether your writing is good or bad. The more people who do not know or care about the language, and the higher up the hierarchy they are, the more rife will be sloppy, badly expressed, ill-punctuated, confusing prose. An Ernst & Young survey in 1993 linked literacy to the cost of lost custom, cancelled orders, over-staffing, unnecessary recruitment. The bill was estimated at £8.4 billion. Plainly, mistakes through misunderstandings cost money; loss of time in trying to understand costs money; and the bad public image that accrues from bad writing may cost a reputation.

9 *Fear of giving offence* Political correctness is laudable where it insists on fairness and truly reflects the modern world. But its excesses are striking at the heart of clear communication. In its desire to rid the language of everything it regards as prejudice, discrimination or bias it is inventing euphemisms which castrate sense. Other words are banned, turning the middle-aged and elderly into a bunch of neurotics. It is harder and harder to say what you mean, and the already written word has frequently to be recast to take gender equality into account.

Political correctness is an important issue for the PR profession. As it is bound up with equal opportunities, racial discrimination, academia and the educational system, you will not be able to avoid it. Not offending your publics is crucial; but so is making yourself understood. If you want to work in local authorities or pitch for a health account you will find that unless you adopt the PC rules you will get neither job nor client.

Books on political correctness list so many unfamiliar phrases in place of single words that you cannot tell which is meant seriously. The main trends are to equalise the sexes and to avoid being disparaging. In a sense, the politically correct movement is being more precise: the informal 'taxman' is being replaced by the two, gender-correct, exact and expressive words 'tax inspector'. The use of terms like 'spastic' (for people with cerebral palsy) and 'mentally handicapped' (for people with learning difficulties) is actively discouraged. 'Cripple', 'handicapped', 'the disabled', 'dwarf', all are words likely to fall into disuse.

The gender battle is being won too. Mankind (human kind), fire-man and stewardess (fire fighter, flight attendant), chairmanship (chairship?) all have the black spot. Even the church now discourages He and Him. You can no longer with impunity write 'he': alternatives like s/he (unpronounceable) and 'he or she' (ugly used even once) are suggested as alternatives. The best solution seems to be to use the singular with the plural. 'Everyone to their taste', 'journalists . . . their' rather than 'journalist . . . his'. The jarring of the singular subject with the plural pronoun is eased because of the modern tendency to think of a team, council, board, company or group not as a single entity but as a collection of people.

The politically correct (or is it culturally sensitive?) movement has one good tip for public relations. It starts from the premise: 'Before we can change a pattern of behaviour, we must change the terms that relate to it.' You cannot think if you have no word to identify the thought; change the word and you change the thought.

10 *Inundated with information* So much information, so little time to absorb it and see if it's useful. The need to skim information is devaluing the written word. As PR people want (favourable) coverage, they will often be happy with a two-page article that is never read (except as a press cutting). So the quality of what is written matters less than that it is published. This in turn leads to what the Americans call refrigerator journalism. The textbite equivalent of the soundbite – information to tear out and keep handy behind the magnet on the refrigerator door.

How to write well

Improving your writing means working at whatever you can identify as the failings in how you write now.

1 *The writing process* Be aware that expressing your thoughts in writing has two separate, alternating stages. First, let your ideas come out in any way that suits you but do not censor them; let your creative thinking have full rein (even on a short memo). Second, analyse, organise and edit what you have produced. Then do some more thinking, then some more revising. Some people do the two processes simultaneously but if you are not a natural writer keeping the two separate should help. Putting the draft away in a drawer for a day and coming back to it helps. You start thinking creatively again when you read what appears to have been written by someone else.

2 *Getting started* Angela Heylin, in *Putting It Across*, recommends reading a couple of pages of a good book. Another approach is called 'free writing': just write down anything that comes into your head and keep going. Some people make notes (use sentences rather than key words), either from their mind or from reference sources.

The main thing is to concentrate on the subject matter and what you want to say.

3 *Hardware* There are hushed tones these days if you say you write with pen and paper! However, you should use whatever is best for you; what works. Scribbling on a pad brings the ideas out direct through the pen, fast. You can cross out and carry straight on; see what you have crossed out, and put it back in; draw arrows to move a paragraph (or cut it out and stick it in a different place). Even having a comfortable, fast-flowing pen helps.

Some people write directly on to a word processor; for you its strength may be as an aid to editing and polishing when you have the material roughly as you want it. Spellcheck is useful, but it will not pick up spelling mistakes that end up as words (manager: manger; their: there). Software has been developed to help with grammar, syntax and expression. But you need to know all that for yourself. Check on screen. Then print what you have written and proof read it as hard copy. It's surprising how differently you feel about it. Proof reading is a necessary skill in PR, and it keeps you in touch with the wording and sense of what you have written.

4 *Study good writing* Study the quality nationals and *The Sun*.
Compare the vocabularies, the length of the words and the sentences. Try typing out some paragraphs from them to get the feel
of the writing. See how it is organised. Compare coverage of the
same story in different papers. Compare different ways of writing
the same thing, like the dinner and event announcements in *The
Times, The Independent* and the *Daily Telegraph*. Your local library
will have these papers if your office doesn't. Cut out different
types of writing from the national and periodical press: news
reports, interviews, feature articles, snippets. Work out how they
are constructed. Note the use of direct speech. Look at beginnings
and endings. Try *The Economist*; it has to be well-written as so
many of the topics are dry. Analyse pages from novelists who
write well. Look at essays and short stories. Read thrillers for a
sense of pace. If you enjoy sport, read the sports columnists on
the quality nationals for how to write humorously.

Use these as your models, not your chairman's statement in the
report and accounts, academic articles, engineering reports written in the passive voice.

5 *Words* George Orwell's classic advice to prefer the short word
to the long, unless it reads awkwardly, still holds true, but only
the tabloids seem to take notice. The problem is that words are
often used in PR to fill out time on television ('at this moment in
time' instead of 'now'), to conceal lack of ideas in articles (roundabout phrases fill up space), to obtain a boss's or client's OK (who
claims that 'manufactured' sounds better than 'made', 'first ever'
sounds better than 'first'). Simple nouns and verbs make quicker
sense. No wonder businessmen want the facts on one sheet of
A4: they can't stand the threat of more pages of management,
marketing or public relations cant. If you are forced to use specific
long words – technical writing abounds with them – make the rest
as short as you can to compensate.

Remember the Allied Forces press conferences broadcast on Sky
during the Gulf War? A 'miss' was called 'incontinent ordnance'
and 'collateral damage' was 'civilian casualties'. Mind, 'rotor heads'
wasn't bad for 'helicopter pilots'. For a while 'attrited', 'to scud'
and 'scenario-dependent' became early morning listening.

Write with nouns and verbs; be sparing and careful in using adjectives and adverbs. This is especially important for press release and information sheet writing where you should concentrate on facts, not superlatives.

Always look unfamiliar words up in the dictionary. This will save you misspelling them, make sure you know the meanings of more words, and it's fun. A search for the definition of 'publicity' will turn up 'puffery', 'pudsy', 'pukka', 'pucker' and 'puce' (flea-coloured) on the same spread.

The computer industry invented a jargon generator in the 1950s; sociology did the same in the 1970s. Here's a PR jargon generator for the 1990s. Take a word from each column to create a useful phrase for your next piece of writing:

key	corporate	communication
basic	leading-edge	strategy
viable	meaningful	methodology
on-going	significant	prioritisation
advanced	state-of-the art	positioning
in-depth	transparent	lifestyle
flexible	user-friendly	parameters
perceived	prestigious	interface
major	definitive	implementation
coherent	relevant	image
pro-active	conceptual	focus

Phrases like 'pro-active, meaningful communication' or 'perceived, conceptual parameters' sound good. No matter that they are meaningless. They proliferate in management, marketing and PR English. Nowadays corporations 'need to restructure their organisations' when all they really need to do is to 'reorganise'. But why write one word when you can write three? If you discover that you are writing like that: stop.

6   *Sentences*   Vary their length and construction. The Plain English people suggest 20 words as the ideal sentence length but there is nothing wrong with some long sentences, with subordinate clauses, if your punctuation makes them easy to understand. The longer the sentence, however, the harder it is to take in all the ideas, and the more likely you are to forget how it began. This is anacoluthia (not a lot of people know that) – when the end of a long sentence ceases to relate to the way it begins. If in doubt, keep sentences short. Avoid jerkiness. Be concise but not abrupt. Too many short sentences leave your prose devoid of rhythm. You cannot write precisely all the time – anyway, that would

remove individuality and style – but avoid a succession of loose sentences.

7 *Use the active voice* 'Aman sent out the press release' is shorter than 'the press release was sent out by Aman' – by 25 per cent. So you cut length by a quarter when you use the active voice. Give the sentence a subject. You could just say 'the press release was sent out' with similar brevity but you would give less information. Sometimes you will want to avoid saying who has been responsible for an action. That's when the passive voice is useful. The passive has a deadening as well as a lengthening effect and is hard to avoid in technical writing. It is what it says, passive.

8 *Avoid repetition* Group similar information together; that will help the reader and make sure you are not repeating yourself. Beware the plodding approach. Such a plodding approach keeps repeating the subject. A plodding approach can be improved by using pronouns, combining sentences. Beware the plodding approach of repeating the subject, when you could use pronouns and combine sentences. Beware, too, the desire to make the same point again using different words.

9 *Paragraphs* A paragraph is for organising your thoughts on one aspect of a topic before going on to another. This will normally mean two, three or four sentences in most documents intended for the press or your boss. But be guided also by length and look of the page: the eye needs a break. *The Sun* uses one-sentence paragraphs partly because it has such narrow columns.

A paragraph will often start with a sentence that sets the scene for the next 50 or 100 words or so. It will often end with a link to the next paragraph.

10 *Edit* When writing a letter to a friend you can be as loose, unsystematic and slipshod as you like: it all adds to the enjoyment. Formal writing is different. It matters to your career what the reader thinks of your approach. So cut out all loose phraseology and unnecessary words unless that spoils the rhythm of your sentences, reads jerkily or appears discourteous.

Journalists edit – sub – because they need to squash more information into a finite space. Get rid of unnecessary phrases that can be replaced by one word ('many' instead of 'a considerable number of', 'when' instead of 'at the time when', 'disagreement' (or 'row' in tabloidese) for 'conflict of opinion', and so on). Remove phrases which do not add to meaning: 'indicated an improvement' instead of 'indicated that there had been an improvement'. Change noun phrases into verbs ('the . . . of the . . . ' is the give-away): 'The organisation of the presentation was a problem' reads more smoothly as 'organising the presentation was a problem' and is 25 per cent shorter. ('A quarter shorter' would sound silly – avoid rhymes, alliteration, absurdity.)

Following those ten suggestions will have a dramatic effect on the clarity of your writing and your ability to simplify anything that is put before you as a draft. Here are some more suggestions:

- Practise
- Prefer familiar words to the far-fetched
- Avoid useless qualifying words (the true facts)
- Avoid clichés and automatic phrases (bad cold, all-time high)
- Avoid tautology (the honest truth)
- Write naturally, not trickily
- Avoid qualifiers (very, somewhat)
- Avoid sloppy spelling (thru)
- Do not explain too much but include all important points
- Avoid awkward adverbs (tiredly)
- Don't be ambiguous (The Greeks the Persians shall subdue). Check for unconscious humour (an 18-year-old girl accused of stealing a jar of vanishing cream has since disappeared)
- Proof-read for literals (a press release on the visit of a party of Indian businesspeople to a town to study transport systems had the phrase 'turban development study')
- Avoid knee-jerk phrases (do not hesitate to contact me)
- Use fresh metaphors: research has shown they increase memorability
- Avoid foreign languages (except where English has absorbed them, as is its habit)
- Choose the right 'setting' for words – *The Sun* might talk of 'being sick', a medical journal of 'regurgitating'. (In USA 'being sick' has a more general meaning)
- Prefer standard words to the off-beat (briefed, obsoleted)
- Define the unfamiliar (which means knowing your audience)
- Put words in the right places (try out 'only')
- Keep the same standpoint: don't go from 'one' to 'you', 'it' to 'they', 'we' to 'I'

- It's best to keep yourself in the background. The reader will know that what you write is your opinion
- Break any rule, as Orwell said, if it reads better.

WRITING BUSINESS LETTERS

'Write as if you believe your correspondent to be intelligent; write as compactly, briefly, simply and directly as you can; keep closely to the point; write as if you are not only responsible for what you write but also responsible for what you do; be polite and pleasant.'
– Eric Partridge

Language shapes the perception of reality as much as it shapes reality
Edward Sapir

The relation between words and things is neither inherent nor permanent so . . . language constructs as well as reflects culture.
Edward Sapir

Punctuation (. , : ; - – "" " ? !)

Have you read a book about pronunciation recently? Why it poses such a problem when it is simply a means of communicating thoughts clearly, is hard to say. Sentences carry ideas and, before there are too many to take in, you put a full stop.

In 'quoted speech' the stop goes outside the quotation marks if the quote is a complete sentence, inside if it isn't.

Commas are to help the sense inside the sentences, representing either a slight mental pause, or visually separating little ideas. Many press release writers forget to comma off subordinate clauses. It's 'Ms Louise Njimba, winner of this year's Great PR award, opened the exhibition' not 'Ms Louise Njimba, winner of this year's Great PR award opened the exhibition.' Use commas a little as possible, keeping them for where they help sense.

Colons and semicolons are misused, confused and ignored. Pity, because they provide great flexibility in writing style. Colons lead you on: what comes after them tells you something promised in the first part of the sentence. It may be a list or an explanation. Unless the wording after the colon forms a completely separate sentence, do not begin it with a capital letter. The American usage is a capital letter: You can see it in their text books and in more recent British newspaper style. The punctuation mark : – , much used last century, is unnecessary because the dash adds nothing to the colon.

Semicolons, on the other hand, make stronger breaks than commas but are not so final as a full stop. You should use them to divide up lists which have long comma'd off phrases, such as photo-captions of several people and their job titles; the semicolon saves the commas being confusing. They can also help counterpoint linked ideas in the same sentence. Too often a semicolon is used instead of a colon. 'Visit; Kew Gardens, Buckingham Palace . . . ' said one journal (instead of 'Visit:').

First typewriters and then computers tried to get rid of the dash – by using a hyphen instead. Newspapers are not keen on too many dashes – they tend to break up narrow columns and bother the eye. But the dash, prudently used, is excellent for adding a thought. Two of them – used either side of an interjection – are a good alternative to brackets. Use brackets for a comment that is a helpful aside; use dashes for a thought a little more distant from the subject matter. (Brackets, and dashes used instead of them, are known as parentheses; commas can be used too, but in the softest way.) Full stops go inside the bracket in stand-alone sentences (and outside when the parenthesis is part of the sentence).

Apostrophes are also a threatened species. Designers hate them; sign makers lose them; even professors of English foretell their doom. Yet the so-called rules that people complain are hard to remember are minimal and logical. To show possession a singular noun takes 's as in: 'the PR department's plans'. If there is more than one PR department then it is s' to show that several PR departments have plans: 'the PR departments' plans'. If the noun is already in the plural you don't need to repeat yourself, thus: 'the children's shirts are longer than the men's'. Because of the apostrophe in it's (it is), the possessive its (its ball) does not have one. What could be simpler?

An apostrophe is also used to show when something is missing: don't (do not); So'ton (Southampton); '95 (1995). When a lot is missing – 'bus (omnibus), 'phone (telephone) – the remains of the word gradually stand on their own in time. Whatever you do, don't use apostrophes to indicate plurals: tomatoe's, the 1990's.

Advice not to over-use the hyphen has been taken to the extent that few PR people seem to know of its existence except as an inferior stand-in for the dash. The hyphen is used to join two words when together they have a distinct meaning. With successful pairings the hyphen tends to drop out over the years: audio visual, audio-visual, audiovisual; life style, life-style, lifestyle. The nuisance is that all three variants are used at the same time; meanwhile, scores of other pairings are also in one of their three stages. Be consistent, and look up what *Hart's Rules* or the house style, house-style, housestyle books say.

The hyphen is used naturally to differentiate between two words that would otherwise look the same (re-cover and recover), to separate vowels in words with prefixes (anti-inflationary, co-operate). Some compound words always take hyphens to show they are a unit: son-in-law, four-year-olds. Sense demands hyphens: white-collar worker; red-wine bottle. Numbers from 21 to 99, when written out, are hyphenated units: thirty-two. Fractions are hyphenated: one-third.

You can use either double or single inverted commas to indicate direct speech, but be consistent. Newspapers vary in their choice while novels, with a lot of conversation, use the single form. When what someone is saying includes a quote from someone else use the alternative form for the inner quote. 'When the PR director spoke to me she said, "Have you a copy of Fowler's *Modern English Usage?*"' It is useful to keep double quotes for speech so that you can also use single quotes to draw attention to an 'oddity' and avoid quotes clashes: 'boys". Avoid the jollity and double-take comment of exclamation marks!

Do you always put a question mark at the end of direct questions? That's the only time they are needed. Don't ask why.

Model your writing on good journalistic style. While they vary on detail the style books of the press show general agreement. *The Economist Style Guide* is excellent because it goes beyond grammar and usage with a fact checker and glossary. Style guides – the rules of consistency applied by individual publications – are published by several news-papers. They are inexhaustible reads and solve such problems as when to use capital letters and how to differentiate between British and American English.

Finally, four aspects of writing often forgotten:

1 *Smart presentation* Check that it looks well on the page: neat, tidy, evenly spaced with sensible margins, pleasing appearance, not

too congested, several paragraphs, and no fancy computer tricks to distract from the text.

2 *Correct format* Make sure it has all the qualities of its genre. If it is a letter, it needs to be properly addressed; if a contact report, bullet points are best and make it easy to see who has to take action on each item; if a detailed report, the summary should be near the beginning and the whole well-structured; if a press release, the story should be in the first two sentences and the rest of the information in descending order of importance.

3 *Crossheads* Use plenty of them. They make it much easier to follow what you have to say. In documents and serious articles they are best as two or three word summaries of what is coming; for newsletters they can imitate the titillating, one-word attention-getters used in the tabloids.

4 *Bullet points* You have to decide when sequential prose is needed and when you should simply pick out the main points and not worry too much about style and grammar:

- short reports
- succinct memos
- lists to break the monotony
- highlighting actions
- short introductions and summaries
- when your boss prefers it.

5.2 *Making presentations*

You will not be able to avoid making presentations. You should not wish to avoid but be the one who wants to make presentations. In a sense, you are presenting yourself all the time: when going for an interview, asking for more money, negotiating, making a telephone call. Your sense of dress, your body language, how you transmit your attitudes, your tone of voice, the way you take part in a conversation, all need to be attended to.

The less successful you are, the more you need to look for the reasons. The way you present yourself can be a reason. First impressions are supposed to be vital. If you are extremely good at something that is badly needed, you may get away with a more relaxed approach. This does not mean that you have to adopt a wholly artificial approach. By all means be natural but at the same time be aware of the context you are in, and of the effect you have on other people, especially in set-piece circumstances like an interview. There is, in PR, always pressure to perform.

Nothing will bring this home better than the discipline of preparing a presentation. The act of thinking out how to get your message across to an audience, and of putting it into practice, is a mirror for seeing the work there is to do when you *are* the message. As with many other aspects of public relations, you need to be able to perform at least adequately, or have a good understanding of the principles, so that you can help others in your organisation with their performances.

If you join a consultancy, sooner or later you will be part of a team that makes a pitch for new business. If you are a young manager, sooner or later you will be presenting a case to your staff, handling team briefings, helping others to communicate. So, who is your audience? And how many of them will there be? How much do they already know about the subject? What are their attitudes likely to be? (Mostly, audiences are on your side from the beginning, wanting you to be good. They want to enjoy themselves, learn and be enthused – not embarrassed. They love good performances. But not too much performance and too little content.)

The nature of your audience and the content of what you have to say, together determine where the presentation takes place, the visual aids needed, your methods and your manner. What is the presentation for? Why are you doing it? To teach, to inform, to persuade, to motivate? This will decide whether you can afford to be informal or need a degree of acting and staginess in how you put your message across. Give yourself plenty of time to prepare what you have to say. A day or two is often not enough. The more work you put into it, the greater the compliment you pay your audience. If you take part obviously ill-prepared and not much bothered, that is the message your audience will receive.

Collect

If you have two or three weeks in which to prepare an important presentation (important to you anyway), use the time to collect bits and pieces of information you might use. Just toss them into a filing box. It is surprising how giving a talk makes you take a wider interest in bookshops, journals, magazines, newspapers, radio and TV programmes, booklets to send away for, illustrative objects, videos, seminars and workshops. When you have a specific aim in mind you notice more of interest than otherwise. If only you could contrive this intensity more often, how well-furnished your mind (or your files or your database) would be.

Because of this it is a constructive habit to open a series of files or box files on topics that interest you, or which you ought to know about for your work. Then you have a head start on the subject of your presentation. For a career in PR you could start files on most of the chapter headings for this book. If you want to be orderly, ring binders with subject sections are the time management recommendation.

Structure

When you have enough material (with what is already in your head) it is time to rationalise it and work out a structure for your presentation. What do you do first; what next; how to end? Where will the examples come? How will you show them? Will the audience be doing any work? Traditional advice over structure is at its most basic in the 'tell them what you are going to say, say it, then tell them what you've told them' school. This is best kept for when you are concerned to get over a few important messages that are to bring about action. An extension of this structure is: grab attention, outline your content, give your central messages, summarise them, end like you began.

Like a story, a presentation has a beginning, a middle and an end. If it hasn't, it is at risk of wandering off into an undergrowth that bemuses audiences. The beginning needs to catch the audience's interest, explaining why they should take notice, establishing your own credibility and authority (or standpoint) and indicating what is to come. The middle is the true content, the argument, the main messages, the examples. The end is the 'close' where you summarise and, if applicable, direct the audience to what is expected of them as a result of what you have said. Or take questions, then summarise.

A more complex version of this is to see the presentation as a three-act play. In Act 1 you outline the situation. In Act 2 you go into the complications – why action is needed. In Act 3 you resolve the drama by proposing answers. This approach has been extended to six steps (which closely resemble report-writing structure): preface, position, problem, possibilities, proposal, postscript.

The words

Unless you are a natural, handling your text will give you the greatest problem. You will go through anxiety states over whether you read it ('I can't *read* it'), memorise it (not recommended even to try) or use file card headings ('But I'll forget the details').

You have to sort out what format will best suit you and your material. But get the text written out first. Work through what you need to say in rough form – no style, no grammar needed. Organise your information along the lines described here and then write it out in good English. Having achieved that, translate the writing into spoken English (more slangy, casual, jerky, friendly, in your personal idiom). This is the secret of writing speeches for others to deliver. Match their rhythms. Use short sentences, concrete nouns, metaphors (which research has shown to be doubly effective).

Go over it and reduce it to key words on a set of file cards, printing at a size you can read at a distance (like on a table top when you are standing). All this work will have bludgeoned a lot of what you have to say into your brain.

Talking

Now you can go off in any one of several directions.

- Just talk to your audience using the file cards as a prompt. Some speakers write key words on their palms.
- Turn your key words into simple statements that can be made into overhead projector acetates or put on 35mm slides. This means your prompts are on a screen and you talk to them. For this not to look too much like a crutch you need some pictorial or diagrammatic material too: photographs, cartoons, statistical tables, charts. Whatever you do, don't just read out the words on the screen.
- If you are really unsure of yourself, type out the text clearly on a PC, double spaced, and read it from a lectern. But don't just read it, appear to be giving a relaxed talk. The trick to this is for the text to be typed in phrasebites suited to your delivery, lines easily memorised for a few moments. Look down, remember the first line, look up and beam the line at your audience, raking them from left to right, or right to left, with an eye-meeting glance. Look down again for the next line (or lines, once you are confident). Some people can do this and make it seem as though they are working from a few notes. The illusion is even more convincing

when you 'know' slabs of the material through rehearsal or familiarity. Anecdotes and examples often only need a key word to trigger your memory. Just as long as you can return easily to where you left off.

- The use of the teleprompt, where you can see the words rolling by in electronic green while your audience is hardly aware of the aid (all they see is a transparent lightweight frame) is best reserved for long and formal speeches. They can produce a metronome-like regimentation of speech and eye contact that hypnotises the audience into disinterest.

- Build your talk around objects (which serve the purpose of prompts). The Christmas lectures from the Royal Institute are a grand-scale example of this with all the experiments and object aids.

- Sometimes two people can present alternately, tossing the ball back and forth.

Five standard equipment aids are available to choose from: overhead projector, flip chart, slide projector, video, whiteboard. You can also use recorded sound. Flip charts are more versatile than might appear because words can be written on them lightly in pencil beforehand to be your prompt. For the audience to see, always write big and practise the lettering. Stand to the side of the flip chart so that you are never with your back to your audience. You can write up your wording on a flip chart beforehand, lightly scoring each sheet at the top so you can tear them off easily to reveal the next. Flip charts and whiteboards are for smallish audiences.

Timing

Timing is your next step. You must rehearse, even if it is by yourself, and time it. Once you have built up plenty of material your problem will be fitting it all in or deciding what to shorten or cut out. If you are one of several speakers you need to have thought about your time being reduced by others over-running. In practice, delivery usually takes longer because of audience reaction or your saying things you have just thought of. It is best not to add to your presentation on the spur of the moment. If you are accepting questions leave time for this and always have extra material ready in case there is silence. (A good speaker may just as easily leave no queries to be raised as stimulate them, so don't worry on that score.)

If you become involved in making the same presentation regularly you will find that you get bored and want to change it, and that new information comes along but you can't fit it all in. Have a clear structure, but allow your memory – with notes beside you as reminders – and the interests of the audience to determine which bits and pieces of information you add in. You don't have to include everything if only a short time is available. Indeed, you won't be able to. So have confidence that the structured theme will bring anecdotes and examples to mind.

Workshops

Be aware of the differences between performing, straight no-frills presentation and teaching. Only perform if you are good at it and sensitive to audience reaction. Otherwise get down to the business and rely on the content being good. If your content is just what the audience needs to hear, as long as you are clear, how you present does not matter much. You can give a three-hour talk, with exercises, sitting down for most of the time. Sitting down means you can have a binder in front of you with notes and reminders, copies of your acetates and exercise material. You don't have to turn your head to look at the screen when you are working with overhead acetates. And you scarcely have to remember a thing. But you will. You will recall comments from previous occasions and find yourself using them.

Alternatively you can be on your feet all the time, interacting with your audience (a U-shape is ideal for this so you can get in among them), asking questions, using their names a lot and generally creating a participative experience. But be sure that they do not feel they are doing all the work.

The venue

Check this out beforehand, especially the technical equipment. Check microphones, height of lecterns in relation to the speaker's height. Harvey Thomas, Mrs Thatcher's advance man, had a retractable-expandable lectern for differently-sized speakers. The only snag was the startling whirring noise it made when changing height.

Your voice

Project your voice to the back of the room but do not shout. Speak clearly and with variation. If you have a flat voice try to do interesting things with it (an imitation perhaps) and vary your pace. Speed up (fast speakers are supposed to be more believable than slow speakers). Slow down for emphasis and deliberate repetition. Punctuate with a video clip or, with small audiences, illustrative objects that can be passed around. If your voice has a habit of cracking up through nerves or bad pitch, drink plenty of water. Contact a voice consultant – actors use them.

Rehearse

If you rehearse (and rehearse and rehearse) and are thoroughly prepared you will be less nervous. And a successful presentation is very good for the ego.

Impromptu

If you are asked to speak on the spur of the moment – at a client dinner, a party, if you have won an award – how do you cope? One victim reached for his wallet and gave an hilarious rendering of the contents: old note reminder to feed the cat (never was fed); condom (in accord with the ethos of the times and crisis PR); credit card, credit card, credit card, credit card, credit card; receipt for . . . you get the idea. A boring wallet might contain notes for a short, impromptu, totally bland speech: . . . like to say have spent an exceptionally enjoyable time at this event, honoured to have been invited, particularly grateful to . . . found especially interesting (the previous speech or the prawn salad or the story told me by a fellow guest who said . . .) great courtesy that you have extended, warm thanks. A less boring handbag might have an anecdote or two, a quotation or two, tucked away inside.

Very short speeches you can cope with in your head if they are based on stories, anecdotes, incidents that would briefly amuse. A little anticipation can save embarrassment. Mark Twain said that it usually took him over three weeks to think up a good impromptu speech. Various famous people, probably Bernard Shaw first, have been attributed with the apology for writing such a long letter, there not having been time to write a short one.

5.3 Media interview technique

If you need one single argument to convince your friends and colleagues of the validity of public relations thinking, the need to organise and manage interviews and TV appearances is it. If you do not prepare, if you appear as your natural, over-frank, twitching, hesitant self, if you do not anticipate, if you do not have your answers ready, if you are dressed inappropriately, all will be lost. Equally, if you do not select the best people to appear, and do not ensure they are trained, you will not be doing your job.

Perhaps twenty or thirty years ago you could do PR knowing little about personal presentation and certainly not expecting to be on television yourself. Now it is so prolific, the world is so tele-visual, if you are in PR you have at the least to know about media presentation and expect one day to be interviewed in your role of communicator or company spokesman. Henry James, who was Harold Wilson's press secretary, used to say: 'Read me only between the lines, see me only behind the camera.' Many of today's company heads of public relations and public affairs believe it is a PR role to speak for the company under many circumstances.

The first step, then, is to become used to making presentations, giving talks. Say a few words at a birthday party, give a talk at a local club or to colleagues in the office, or be the one to introduce a speaker, just so you can experience what it is like, what you need to do to improve. Read books on the subject and try out the advice. If you are in public relations you are expected to be a competent, confident communicator. (You may not be, you may be naturally shy, but you will be expected to be confident, so practise.) Teach yourself. Make your mistakes on the small stage to avoid making any when you face a big audience.

Once you are reasonably articulate on a subject, have friends ask you questions and listen to – tape – your responses. You'll hate your voice (everyone does). In these days of domestic camcorders you may even have the equipment to dummy up a short 'television interview'. Is your voice too loud? Too harsh or shrill? Modulate it – but not to the extent that Mrs Thatcher's advisers went. Do you hesitate a lot, er and um? Did you put the answers across well? Were your mannerisms irritating? Was your appearance OK? Let your friends criticise you – enjoy it, because it is constructive.

This experience alone puts you in a good position to rehearse speakers who are giving a lecture or an address at a press conference. Even if you are not too good at giving talks yourself, you are on a par with anyone else as part of an audience: aware that the speaker sways about, uses their hands distractingly, reads stiltedly, mis-uses visuals.

Being interviewed on a subject you know inside out is really only like answering questions at the end of a talk. In most cases all interviewers want is information that fills time constructively for their programmes.

Radio

You are far more likely to come in contact first with radio interviewing than television. Indeed, you should set out to gain that experience first, even if it is only accompanying a colleague to the studio (which gives them moral support and should lessen their anxiety).

Arrive early – by, say, half-an-hour – become familiar with the background, try to talk to the interviewer first if that's possible, but at least find out the first question to be asked. You will probably be at a table with a microphone pointed at you (ignore it), sitting opposite the interviewer. Behind a glass screen will be the producer and equipment. Sometimes the journalist will come to you, at a press conference perhaps, with portable equipment. Essentially, there's no difference. Many programmes nowadays are made up of voices coming and going against a background of noise designed to give a sense of place, so you could even be shouting over the sound of factory machinery.

It doesn't matter what you look like, or what you are wearing. By the same token, your explanatory gestures cannot be seen either. You can have (short) notes in front of you (big printing). But you must know your subject already and have the main points you want to get across – say three – firmly in mind, perhaps pinned there with a simple three-letter mnemonic. Behave as if you are having a conversation with the interviewer – the trainers will tell you to talk as if to one particular person (say a friend) rather than to the mass audience out there. It's certainly less intimidating.

You must, however, take your best voice with you. It should be expressive, varied, controlled. There is an entertainment element in broadcasting. People listening or watching usually relax more than if they are reading for information. They are probably less critical too. All you have to worry about is sound. So avoid ers and ums, tapping the table, having your mobile phone or pager in your pocket, bleeping an alarm from your wrist half-way through, or rustling notes.

If you are doing a phone-in, the only differences are that of a lot of people will be asking questions (but more for advice) and you will be on air live, not being recorded for editing. Be well-prepared, with all the statistics to hand, and imagine all the questions you can, or you will not be convincing.

Breathing

Voice and breathing control can be learned from specialists. In interviews, avoid dropping your voice or pausing for breath near the end
of a sentence – in case the interviewer thinks you have finished and
interrupts.

TV

The nearest TV to a radio interview is probably the on-line broadcast.
A large audience is going to judge your organisation from how the
interview comes across, but you can't see them. You will probably be
in a small studio somewhere local, linked only by an earphone and not
even able to see the interviewer. You will be one of those talking heads,
beamed through space and looking rather perplexedly out at millions of
viewers.

The pace of these exchanges is less fluent because, having heard yourself introduced, you will be listening carefully over the link for questions
and be looking at the camera lens in your studio. You should sit forward,
look alert and not glance away (for fear of seeming shifty). But you can
have notes in front of you as they won't show.

Answer the question, and stop. Answer the next question, and stop.
A golden rule of being interviewed is to say only what is important,
and then stop. Let the interviewer fill the space.

If you follow much of the training advice that is given, you won't be
answering any questions at all; you will be making your own statements.
This contrived response ruins many interviews for viewers and is only
necessary in extreme situations. Once you watch television reporting
critically, as you must to teach yourself about it, you become aware
of the training. Angela Heylin quotes Brian Walden's analysis of Mrs
Thatcher's ability to evade: ignore the question or acknowledge it but
don't answer or treat it as irrelevant; question the question (a reminder
of the famous Harold Wilson exchange: 'Prime Minister, why do you
always answer a question with a question?' 'Why do you ask that?');
attack the question or the interviewer; make a different point; answer
only in part but as though that was the complete answer; repeat a
previous answer; or make out that the question has already been
answered.

Leaders emerge from important meetings smiling and often go to a
waiting car (they are taught not to run and a car gives them somewhere
to go). 'Please let me finish . . . ' has become a standard interview

ingredient. Only if an interview promises to be adversarial do you need to bring interviewer-controlling training into play. Unless you are involved in a crisis and damage limitation (when you must expect hard-nosed treatment) or something is political (always adversarial, regret-tably) or pressure-group-driven, it is more effective to use TV training to help you communicate, be street-wise and confident in a view or a soundbite. Trying to grab the interview from the interviewer is usually a viewing turn-off and an admission of defeat.

However, many experts (like Brian Tidman and John Brand) will tell you *never* to trust television at any time, never to drop your guard (that's true) and to answer the question with what you want to say in the first few words. Certainly you must decide beforehand what you want viewers to know and how you can best express your organisation. John Brand, in his training, will allow only positive statements.

One of the many fears about being on the wrong side of the television screen is of being distorted and misrepresented. If your contribution is being recorded, two hours may be spent obtaining a minute in the programme. (You may well ask how much money and time is wasted.) From your point of view this is far too long and could lose control of what you think is important. But if you make mistakes you can stop and begin that part again, which you can't do live. You can summarise, which influences the producer in which parts to use. If you make a genuine factual error you can probably persuade the producer to re-record (but not if they think you are covering up). You said it, and you should only say what you know to be so and want to tell. It is important to know how long the final version will be so that you can organise what you say to suit. Tricks have been played by interviewees before now: if you know a two-sided discussion will last three minutes you can time it and come in with your central message after about two minutes forty seconds.

Live

Live interviews cannot be distorted except by yourself – if you are not prepared, or do not give your message early on (and succinctly) or you let the interviewer lead you somewhere you do not want to go. If you think a competitor may be involved in the programme, try to appear live.

Soundbites

In the same way that when you write a press release you need to get all the main points over in the first paragraph, so you have to encapsulate your central message in just a few words. Soundbites figure prominently in news bulletins and are sought from passers-by, victims' relatives, editors, professors, specialists, bosses, analysts, economists and managers alike. They are the 10–30 second pertinent comments sought by television to add colour, balance and verity to their reporting. So, concise English please. Clarity and a positive, creative contribution to what they want. Nothing bland. Know the length they want and speak to time. With due warning (unless you are accosted on the street or the station) you can polish and rehearse and make a success of your first screen appearance.

Doorstepping

This is when a crew descends out of the blue. The stock advice is to stand still (otherwise you may be filmed apparently being evasive). But an alternative is to try to have a logical form of words ready. Experience in providing a response which gives nothing away but satisfies the pursuers (who are only doing their job) is something to make sure you get from TV training. Like a short speech for any occasion, a form of words is worth having in your head. 'The meeting is several days away and it would be wrong of me to anticipate the decision.' 'Well, as you know yourself only too well, there isn't any point in speculating.' 'We are always in talks with other companies as you can well appreciate. There's nothing specific I can tell you right now. No, as I've said, I can't be specific right now. You'll have to wait and see.' 'I'm sure you wouldn't expect me to say anything when the matter is *sub judice.*' Such weasel words at least avoid 'No comment' (which can be taken to be concealment) and give some sort of reason for not co-operating fully. Ordinary people have difficulty using the one from the Palace: 'We can neither confirm nor deny . . . ' Bear in mind that the way you treat reporters conditions how they treat you.

The studio

In your early days in PR try to find some ways of visiting a TV studio, so it does not come as a culture shock at the wrong time. IPR regional groups arrange visits to local TV stations from time to time when a tour is usually offered after a talk. This way you can see how news and other programmes are put out. Write to TV companies and try to be part of a programme audience. Accompany a manager who is going to be interviewed and try to get a flavour of the studio floor, the wires, the busyness and movement, lights, cameras, and floor manager's signals (hand across throat: finish). Take any opportunity of talking to a radio or TV journalist about the background to their work.

You may never be in the hot seat yourself, but your advice will be expected and that much more credible and useful because of your familiarity with the subject.

Interviewer guide

The BBC brought out revised guidelines on interviews in 1990. These are some of the main points made, from the *interviewer's* point of view:

- Have a clear, specific journalistic purpose, obvious to viewers and listeners
- Interviews are for: description, exposition, to test argument, to complain, to find new evidence, or all of those
- Interviewers may: prompt, challenge, say nothing
- Interviewers must be well-prepared, not allowing a 'competent interviewee to sweep them aside'
- When rigorously testing the arguments of people in power, the emotion should come from the interviewee, not from the interviewer (who should be tough-minded, sharp, sceptical and informed, not partisan)
- 'All interviews on contentious matters should be uniformly testing'
- Evasion should be exposed
- 'In a well-conducted interview, listeners and viewers regard the interviewer as working on their behalf'
- 'Interviewers have to contend increasingly with professional and trained interviewees who are skilled at filibustering.'

General advice for the interviewee

- Always assume you are on air until you are outside the building
- Nothing is off the record
- For television, wear clothes that aren't distracting. No small checks or glaring, irrelevant accessories
- Look at the interviewer, not the camera. On-line is the only exception
- Never lose your temper – it means loss of control

- Put the positive first, so the negative is in context
- Make sure your body language is neutral, not a give-away or misrepresenting you simply because you are nervous
- Pick up on important mistakes by the interviewer immediately. But, as Lord Gormley said, let little things go
- Learn to be expressive with your eyes as well as your voice
- Don't interrupt and don't befriend the interviewer by name, it sounds sanctimonious
- You don't have to accept the interviewer's description of the situation, you can rephrase it in your answer and get your main point over
- Have a suitable form of words ready for the worst questions you can be asked, even if it is a deflective answer. 'Your words, not mine. My view is . . . '
- A light manner keeps control
- Mention known supporters if you are challenged
- Attract attention by using the word 'you', be interesting, describe in images, leave a message
- Avoid jargon: use simple words (viewers are supposed to be 12-year-olds). Be natural
- Get straight to the point. To begin with say what you want to say, whatever the question.

Making the decision

But should you agree to an interview? Find out what is wanted, what the programme is, whether it is live or recorded, a solo interview or with others, how long it will be, when it will be, if the audience is of use to you as a public. You don't have to agree. It may be safer not to take part. On the other hand, you may miss an opportunity to get your message across, or concede one to the competition. One of the objectives of most PR work is to have the organisation regarded as a source for informed comment, whether in the press or broadcasting. If you turn down the chance, you may not be given another. On the other hand, do not walk into the lion's den. Do not appear, and do not let colleagues appear, if you judge that the organisation will suffer from the exposure.

TOP SECRET

During the dispute about Sunday opening a reporter rang the local supermarket manager to ask if it would be open on Sundays. However, someone had banned anyone except PROs from speaking to the press, even on simple factual matters:

'Hello, I'm from the *Advertiser* and I'd like to know if you're open on Sunday.'

'I'm not allowed to tell you.'

'What do you mean?'

'I'm not allowed to speak to the press. You'll have to go through the press office.'

'Are you allowed to speak to the public?'

'Yes.'

'OK then: I'm a member of the public. Are you open this Sunday?'

'Yes'

REPORTER RELATIONS

In June 1994 there was a fire at a hotel in Windsor. This was of news relevance only because of its proximity to the castle (which had had its own well-publicised blaze). A reporter rang the press office for the hotel group, who duly promised to get some details. A short while later a statement was issued giving details of the fire itself but none of the background information about the hotel, innocuous details such as when it was built, how many rooms it had and the cost of a night's stay.

'What about the background I asked for?' said the reporter.

'That's our statement,' said the press officer.

Thinking there must be a misunderstanding, the reporter asked again but got the same answer. Even when asked for reasons, the press officer, after several embarrassed silences, stuck to the prepared statement and refused to give background details – which the reporter then found out from other sources.

6

SKILLS:PRACTICAL
——— EXPERIENCE ———

6.1 Media relations

The media are the press, and television and radio broadcasting – the main means of mass communication. Coverage in the media is usually one of the prime aims of public relations (but some organisations do not like to be talked about. The British Royal family knows the feeling.) Media relations vary from extreme antagonism to friendly collaboration, from overkill to disinterest and treachery, from a distant accord over news, issues and information to a gossip machine that runs out of control.

You should always know why you want coverage. You should always know what you are doing and whom you are dealing with. You should not promise – guarantee – coverage; you are not in advertising.

Journalists want stories. In February 1994 Norman Lamont, no longer Chancellor of the Exchequer, survived two taped interviews with Ginny Dougary only to say what he really thought over lunch. A specialist writer for a national paper, attending a press conference on your premises, is allowed to make a phone call from a director's office; a confidential file is open on the desk. Christine Keeler, door-stepped by a journalist when some of the Profumo papers were released in 1994, said: 'I have had 30 years of this. Let me get my life together. Please just leave me alone . . . I don't want the world to know where I live.' Quotable quote in *Today*. You can't quote silence or absence, though you can report it. Hence the fear of 'No comment' being interpreted as something to hide. Instead you need a form of words that says something but gives nothing away.

It depends who you are. The prime minister's press secretary is perhaps in for a harder time than the PRO for Anodyne Products Limited. It depends on how well-informed you are. You are less likely to be caught out if you have knowledge of a situation. Never drop your guard with a journalist; but do forge trusting relationships; and always be prepared.

Public relations people often claim their work is far more than 'just media relations' but most straw polls will show a good 60 per cent of their time is spent on it. Organisations want favourable coverage.

As a press officer your work will depend on the nature of the organisation you are with. Large, well-known organisations and national institutions (like the BBC) do not have any trouble gaining coverage. They have trouble gaining the coverage they want and avoiding the coverage they don't want. Small, everyday businesses have the opposite problem. How on earth can they get 'a mention'? Journalists' complaints about receiving too many press releases containing 'puffery' are the result of PR people trying too hard. But they are often hired by their masters to 'get us into the papers' and if they say they can't, what price staying in the job?

Some pointers to help you with your media relations, your contact with the media and your relationships with them:

- Study closely and regularly the media and the journalists that are important to you. There are all sorts of nooks and crannies where your information might be lodged.
- Realise that journalists are different, work for different parts of the media which each have their own characteristics. Local press, radio, regional daily, industrial correspondent, *Sun* reporter, political columnist, diary editor, technical journal or consumer magazine editor, specialist correspondent: all different.
- Look at the information you have from the journalist's point of view. Your management won't.
- Do not join the army of PROs who look down on journalists as an inferior race who are expected to realise that you control the information they want. You will make enemies. Anyway, the best ones will be more intelligent and well-informed than you; it's just that journalism doesn't pay so well as PR.
- Remember that journalists have to start somewhere too. And they

change jobs. The tyro on *Chartered Surveyor Weekly* may shortly be the property correspondent for the *Daily Telegraph*.

- Go to endless trouble to provide the right information at the right time.
- Learn to write competently; gain respect.
- To build acquaintanceship with journalists you need to 'bring something to the party'. The relationship is symbiotic. Journalists and PR people need each other but, as a fact of life, often dislike and mistrust each other's function.
- All communication with journalists is two-way. Once you have opened up the contact there is no hiding when it is inconvenient for you to answer their questions. You are now one of their contacts.

It is easier to talk to someone you know than to a stranger. But there is always a first time. In any case, the test is: do you have a story? Or, if you don't, have you something to offer that will be of use to the journalist? A background meeting with a specialist in your organisation is ideal.

Get to know your trade and local press editors and writers. You are new to the job. Learn as much about it as possible in a short time and make contact with the media around you. It can be a short phone call, an evening drink, a quick lunch: find out at first hand what each journalist is interested in from your organisation. Then you can burrow away at providing it.

One of the best ways of meeting journalists for the first time is at a press conference or on a plant visit. If you can be on hand when they sign in, so much the better. There are people who regard themselves as lifelong acquaintances of anyone they have spoken to once on the phone. Think what deep relationships they have with journalists met for a fleeting moment at the press conference reception desk.

One of the benefits of joining a largish PR consultancy is that you benefit from the experience and contacts of others. When extra people are needed at a press conference or an event, volunteer.

Passing on information

- *Write a letter*   Work out your idea and put in a short, highly organised letter to the journalist. Follow up by telephone a few days later.

- *Make a phone call*   Have a note beside you of the main points. Keep your conversation short and to the point. Try to sell the idea in 30 seconds. They can only say no. Sometimes they will be rude, but rarely. Mostly they will ask you to develop the idea in writing so they can make a less pressurised decision. Learn when to ring and when to write. It depends on lead times, industry sectors, complexity, importance.

- *Send a fax*   The more immediate the need for information, the more appropriate the fax machine is. A 1993 survey by Grice Wheeler, publishers of the *Guide to European Business Media*, found that 86 per cent of international newsrooms favoured fax. That seems logical, it's like being next door to a newspaper office in Turkey or Australia. Most of the time, however, a fax is over-kill – you would only fax a monthly or a quarterly if you were right up against its deadline. You can never be certain a fax has gone through (whatever the digital display tells you) or to the right place. Anyway, newspaper offices are busy and faxes easily go astray, rolling straight across the floor and into the wastepaper basket.

- *Send a press (media) release*   This is still the conventional, and simplest, method of sending out the same information to several media outlets when the deadline is not same day (or even, by media distribution services like Two-Ten Communications and PIMS which use their own couriers, when it is). Press releases should be as short and tightly written as possible, contain only relevant information, and start with the important points (who, what, where, when, why). See page 159 for how to write a press release (which is not a literary or art form of singular importance but simply a conventional means of passing information).

- *Electronic connections*   You can pay companies like Two-Ten and PIMS to send your information out through their electronic links to media computer screens. More and more information will pass electronically in future. Already it is the preferred way for company results to be received by the Stock Exchange.

- *Journalist meeting*   Arrange for an interested journalist (who you know is responsible) to visit your organisation, see round it, speak to key people, lunch with a specialist and a representative of management. Where it is important for the organisation to be understood, a regular programme of familiarisation lunches helps orientate everyone. If you have a story, even better. If you want journalists to contact your organisation when they want comment on an issue, this increases the chances.

Sometimes a lunch, or just a meeting, with two or three journalists from media that do not compete with each other, is a good solution. A local paper, a trade journal, a specialist freelance and a radio journalist could be effective.

- *Special meetings* Sometimes you can get small groups of people who have common interests together for lunch or dinner, with a guest speaker. This can allow you to mix your own people, your suppliers, associates, someone you want to be in contact with, an outside specialist and a journalist (as long as everyone knows who is going and the basis of the discussion).

- *Press conferences* Keep these for important announcements when journalists will benefit from being able to question your organisation's leaders and specialists. When news breaks, conferences are held at short notice; even, if the story is running continuously (as with a crisis), at fixed times every day. Normally, however, you will want to give about three weeks' notice and plan the proceedings carefully. Press conferences deal with a topic all at once and get it over with. They need forward planning, an appropriate venue and full rehearsal. They are sometimes turned into stagey occasions with slideshows, presentations, demonstrations. The test: is it worthwhile the journalist coming? Could the information have been given better in some other way?

- *Write an article* Apart from the straight information and background notes they supply, PR people spend their lives trying to persuade journalists to write stories for them. But there are many opportunities to write articles (which gives you control of the ideas). Study the media outlets for such opportunities. Many trade press journals will take knowledgeable (not sales-driven) pieces from specialists in your organisation. Don't think news, think background, think 'interesting'. Special features on given topics are common throughout the media; tap into them with a by-lined article. Many short-staffed editors welcome well-written, informative contributions as long as they are not too product orientated.

- *Write a letter to the editor* A short, to-the-point letter to the editor is a way of entering a debate, starting a debate, countering a wrong impression, or just attracting a little attention to your organisation. Editors are more sensitive to balancing coverage nowadays because they do not want to be thought prejudiced against a minority interest. Don't get disheartened; always be relevant.

- *Media tour* If you have a story that will last for a week or two, and a credible, well-informed spokesperson who has the time, a tour of regional media can be highly effective. By moving into a chosen geographical area you can get round many of the local free-sheets, weeklies, regional dailies, radio and television stations. This will work best with concepts and high consumer interest topics: for instance, health, nutrition, safety.

- *Radio tapes* You can record an interview with your spokesperson and send tapes to the local radio stations. If it appeals, they may use the tape. If it is just a blatant product plug, they won't. A creative approach, worked out from a journalistic and regional point of view, works best. You will need advice and help from the company producing the tapes. Tapes can be organised and syndicated with gaps so that the local interviewer can ask the questions (the answers being on the tape).

- *Video news releases (VNRs)* Generally, television does its own filming. The TV stations do not want to carry material that might prejudice their independence. But this is changing with the times and certainly if you have a biggish budget and a topic high in visual interest, VNRs can be successful. Footage may be used to show context (if the subject is something rather inaccessible in practice, or startling and immediate). VNR material kept as background in the organisation's crisis suitcase could suddenly become important.

CASE STUDY

DHL Everest 40 Expedition

The international couriers, DHL, have an advertising catchphrase: 'Ain't no mountain high enough'. To promote themselves as a global carrier DHL sponsored a climb of Mt Everest by a British woman. They used Nepalese runners and helicopters to get pictures and video film footage back quickly from Everest to DHL carriers who took them to London, where the film was turned into VNR material. A satellite solar telephone was used for direct communication with the expedition.

The VNR material was aired continually on virtually every national news programme broadcast in the UK, and incorporated into news and documentary programmes and chat shows. This Shandwick Sponsorship campaign won the special programmes category in the IPR's 1994 Sword of Excellence Awards.

TELEVISING LUCY

The Engineering Council's Young Engineers for Britain competition is bringing a better understanding of technology into the classroom. Hundreds of young people aged from 11 to 19 invent their own devices or enter examination projects, competing for prizes of £20,000.

Sixteen-year-old Lucy Porter from Bath won the title of 1993 Young Engineer for Britain and the pictures of her playing on the swing she had invented for disabled children were widely used by the national and provincial press, Fig. 6.1. However, Ron Kirby, director of public affairs for the Council, realised there was an outstanding story in the enthusiasm of the contestants and the amazing range of their inventions; he handled the attempt at television coverage in an unusually ambitious way. He hired a TV news crew and then fed coverage of the event through to seven BBC and ITV regional television companies who were interested because students from their area were taking part. He assumed that London TV stations would probably send their own crews.

On the day the entries were judged, TV companies were offered a package comprising an interview with Ron Kirby and interviews with local contestants. When the results were announced, a similar package was offered: an interview with the Council's director general, coverage of the awards ceremony, and interviews with local contestants. The service was free of charge apart from the relatively minor cost of booking lines from the BT tower, from where the material was distributed. Seven local TV stations out of the 19 approached took feeds. Filming was done by a team from the independent company TV News London and the video tape rushed back to their Millbank base for editing. The 15-minute packages, tailored to local requirements, were sent out in the afternoon by facilities house Walshys in time for early evening news programmes. Advance press releases were sent to news desks and the Engineering Council kept in touch with station contacts. Filming the day before the winners were announced helped, because several stations taking reports about their local entrants came back next day when the winners were known. The Engineering Council then used the footage to make a video to help promote the 1994 competition.

Fig. 6.1 Lucy and the swing she designed for disabled children

Embargoes

An embargo asks that information is not used before a specific time. A few journalists ignore embargoes as a matter of course (best learn who they are in your line of work). The main occasions when an embargo is essential are: to control the timing of an announcement in relation to journalists' deadlines and different international time zones; and to give journalists time to absorb a large mass of information (like a complex annual report).

Do not use an embargo to make your story seem more important or for the convenience of your organisation. You can easily send out information on different dates to suit the publication deadlines of dailies, weeklies and monthlies. If a journalist asks you for more details about embargoed information, cover yourself by saying that what you say also comes under the embargo. Similarly, make clear that any broadcast interview relating to an embargoed story must not be used before the time stated. To avoid radio jumping the gun, the embargo time should be the end, not the beginning, of a press conference. Whatever you do, don't use an embargo to give an exclusive to one or two 'mates'.

You destroy trust if you restrict most journalists but let others have an edge.

Embargoes: Dos and don'ts.

- Never impose restrictions or conditions if they can be avoided
- Use embargoes only to ensure equal opportunity among journalists with different deadlines or working across time zones
- Time embargoes to coincide with the event, announcement, launch, publication, or completion of speech – or, in other circumstances, to suit the majority of the appropriate media. Keep the embargo period to a minimum consistent with its purpose
- Embargo any radio or TV interview given prior to a press conference. The press publication time given in an embargo applies equally to broadcasting time
- Never break or vary an embargo to favour or suit the convenience of the few, or leak embargoed information through a third party
- Strictly observe Stock Exchange rules in all matters relating to public companies. Comply with the Company News Service requirements. Also take care to observe any other codes of practice which may refer to the use of embargoes
- Do not give advance reportable information concerning an embargoed story unless it is similarly embargoed
- Be precise about what is reportable, and what is not, in any background briefing.

Off the record

These are not words that journalists wish to hear. Their lives are about stories, not censorship, and their untrammelled reporting is a vital safeguard for the public interest. The words 'this is off the record' must be spoken in advance, not as an afterthought; they are most wisely used with a trusted (and not forgetful) journalist who needs to understand the position better. Otherwise, the best advice you can give your spokesperson or client is: only give information that can be reported.

If it is OK for something to be reported, as long as the source is not identified, then make this clear from the beginning.

Press packs

These give journalists a selection of information in one folder. Plastic wallets will do in a hurry. Not-too-elaborate board folders with a pocket, printed on the cover with the organisation's logo and some significant but timeless details on the inside, are better but more costly. They can be used in many other circumstances and do present the organisation professionally. Typical contents might be:

- The news story
- Captioned photographs
- Background details; fact sheets
- Relevant printed literature.

The texts of speeches delivered at a press conference are best handed out separately as journalists leave. Of course, include them in press packs being sent to journalists who were not able to come.

Press conference arrangements

When? In two to three weeks' time when the news is to break and your people are available. (Unless it's an instant news conference.)

How many from the media will come? Fewer than you would like. It could be embarrassing.

Where? A venue (original or conventional) that will take the number you want to attend plus the 'home' team, is easy for the media to reach, is appropriate to the reason for holding the conference, and has all the services you need.

Programme content. What is to be said, how it will be got across (press pack content, speeches, slides, video?), how long it will take, who is to be there.

Programme logistics. Staffing, catering, equipment, microphones, telephones for journalists without mobiles.

Send out invitations. About three weeks beforehand. A simple letter usually, but may be a printed card or 'teaser'. Always make it easy to answer: a reply-paid or stamped and addressed postcard, or a tear-off slip and stamped and addressed envelope are best.

Check out the venue. Make arrangements for: direction signs, tent cards (with the names of platform speakers nice and large), print, visuals, display board material, photography, refreshments.

Rehearse. Go over the sequence and what is to be said several times. Don't believe it will be OK on the day without rehearsal.

Questions and answers. Think up all the questions that could possibly be asked (the nastier the better), and make sure the speakers have good answers.

Organise your team. Go over all the jobs to be done before, on and after the day of the conference.

Shortly beforehand ring up all the journalists who have not replied to your invitation. Many won't: they are not discourteous, just busy and may indeed not know whether they can come or not until the day itself. Double check with your contacts at the venue and the caterers. Double check with the 'home' team: distribute details of the programme to everyone.

Dangers. The mikes or lights or slide projector won't work. You need an electrician on the spot. Noises off: building work will suddenly appear inside or outside the venue and the pneumatic drills start up. Caterers will play tunes with the cutlery and plates. Another event booms through from an adjacent room. The hotel band strikes up.

The unexpected. Overnight the doors have been removed from your venue rooms. Something that was there last night isn't now. Fire alarm rehearsal. Power failure. Other news may break on the day, diminishing your audience.

Timing. Arrive early. Hold a dress rehearsal. Check everything. As journalists arrive and sign in, give them badges, coffee, soft drinks, press packs. After the presentation (20–30 minutes say), allow for questions.

Photography and photo calls

Become familiar with the work, methods and charges of several photographers. Find out what they are good at. Photographers working on the papers, at local or national level, can be worth getting to know.

There are several recurring circumstances for which you need to be photographically prepared:

- People receiving awards
- Speakers at seminars, press conferences, the AGM
- Visitors to offices and factories
- Photo-calls (you need your own pictures, whoever turns up from the media)
- Product shots in the studio and on site
- Pictures for newsletters, house magazines
- Mug shots of management for appointment releases.

For the kind of photograph that might make the papers, you will need help. If you have what you think could be a photo-story, talk about the possibility of an exclusive to the picture editor of the newspaper that seems most appropriate. Get to talk to picture editors anyway, to find out what they want. (They don't want machine-copied pictures for a start.) If you strike lucky, the photographer the paper uses may help you plan a good visual. Photo-opportunities need creative thinking if they aren't naturally news. Here is an example:

WHY DO YOU ALWAYS FIND JUST ONE?

Fig. 6.2

BT wanted visual coverage of their support of the New Contemporaries Exhibition, an avant-garde travelling exhibition launched at the Government Galleries in Manchester. The venue was a difficulty because London-based newspapers do not easily feature provincial cities except in the local editions. The exhibits in the gallery, perversely, would not make the right picture, nor would the award ceremonies with artists standing by their work. But one young artist who had won a main prize had collected shoes picked up from city streets over some years and cast them in stone. Here was the opportunity for an intriguing image. Stewart Goldstein of Eyecatchers Press working for *The Independent*, took the shot and the project typified the way one unusual picture can give a twist to an idea. It was an artist standing in front of her work – nearly a ton of it – but in a rather different way.

When sending out a photo-call invitation letter, be sure that the time, place, subject and purpose are crystal clear. Have your own photographer present, preferably a freelance press photographer.

Writing a press release

From the way they talk, some PR people think of the press release as a significant publishing achievement, akin to issuing a national newspaper every day. A good press release is hard to write but no great literary achievement. It is just one of the ways of passing information to journalists. As nearly all press releases end up unused – that's what journalists say anyway – it will pay you to make it as good as it possibly can be: short, in journalistic style, factual, spelt correctly and well laid out.

Standard information

- Make it clear on whose behalf the release has been produced
- Date it
- Include a contact telephone number at the end for further information (home as well as work and, if embargoed until a Monday, over the weekend)
- Put more/ . . . or cont/ . . . at the foot of all but the last page.

Printed design

Print the organisation's logo, name, address, phone and fax numbers at the top of the A4 page, leaving as much room as possible below for information. Print 'Press release', 'Media release', 'News release' or 'News and information' at the top too.

If you must have some extra motif (to make the press release more noticeable) do it so there is no interference with the wording.

Text layout

- Always double space to leave room for journalists or subs to change your wording. Single space background notes. Have generous margins.
- Copy newspaper style for indents: none for the first paragraph but indent the rest.
- Many PR people follow traditional practice and put 'ends' to show there are no more sheets. But putting details of someone to contact has the same effect.

Writing the release

- Use as few words as possible – the less work you leave for subs, the better

- What and Why and When and How and Where and Who
- Include the essence of the story in the first two sentences. Don't lead up to it slowly: give the news straight away. Have all the important points in the first two paragraphs – very often that is the most that is likely to be printed
- Then put the rest of the information in descending order of importance. The story is most easily cut from the bottom up
- Keep to the facts. Avoid promotional adjectives and subjective judgements
- A direct quote from an expert or the CEO or senior manager lends colour. This is the place for opinion. But do not put trivial, self-congratulatory phrases in the mouth of your spokesperson; give them something striking to say (or report something interesting they did say)
- It is better to send a journalist one sentence that is useful than ten that are not
- You cannot go wrong by using simple words and punctuation. A press release is not a feature article but a piece of information
- The headline should tell the journalist plainly what the story is about
- Check all spelling and grammar on every draft. You don't want to emulate the press release that read: 'the heir to the thrown' or another which talked about 'column centre metres'
- Double check that all information is accurate and that names are correctly spelt. Releases with mistakes in them do nothing for your credibility either with your organisation or the media. A PR consultancy once sent out a release during a crisis which said their client had nothing to hide. The release was followed by a telephone call saying it was a mistake and must not be used
- Have someone else read it over
- Make sure your boss or client approve the final wording
- Do not treat press releases as experiments in your word processor's typographical versatility.

Distribution

- Unless you send your press release to the right media (correctly addressed) you have been wasting your time
- You can handwrite the envelope, type labels, photocopy from a master sheet on to labels, have your computer print out the addresses or get one of the distribution companies to do it all for you. It doesn't matter as long as the cost is right for the job and the thing gets there
- Use fax when the first class post will be too late. There is hardly

ever any point in faxing to quarterly or monthly journals exc
near copy deadlines. Fax is ideal for international distribution
- Try not to send blank sheets of paper (headed 'important nev
  from . . . ')
- Gradually papers and journals are being set up to take releases by
  E-mail, direct from one computer to another.

Captions to photographs

- Always caption photographs
- The commonest way of overlooking this is when you are asked for
  an individual photograph. At least write on the back to identify the
  image. The point is that if it is mislaid or confused with other
  uncaptioned pictures something nasty might happen
- Three ways of captioning photographs; see Fig. 6.3.

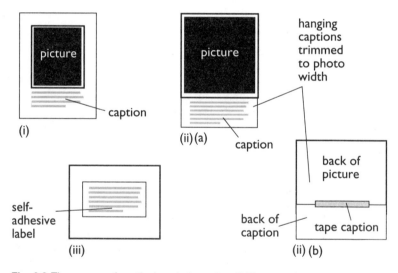

Fig. 6.3 Three ways of captioning photographs: (i) Photograph mounted on sheet
bearing caption; (ii) (a) Hanging caption, trimmed to picture width (b) Caption taped
to back of photograph; (iii) Caption on self-adhesive label on back

Deadly warnings

- Do not fold photocopied captions so that they face the photograph
  – the electrostatic ink can come off on the image
- Don't write on the backs of photographs with those popular Pilot

Hi-Techpoint pens; their ink dries very slowly on photographic paper, nor press hard with ball-point
- Do not use paper clips to attach compliments slips to photographs or transparencies; they may cause damage
- Always use hard-backed envelopes to protect posted photographs.

Writing articles

- Begin with an interesting first sentence idea
- Keep the reader interested
- Group like information together and organise it well
- Use direct quotes to add life and colour
- Follow the beginning, middle, end pattern
- Use lively imaginative, colourful, practical words, not ones that are vague, abstract, long or boring
- Use crossheads to guide the reader and break up the columns
- Follow the principles of writing well.

New media

With electronic media it is important to keep abreast of developments, even if the ideas and initial costs are sometimes ahead of market practicality. Prestel, Ceefax and Teletext are now well understood and used. Other newcomers are:

- *BBC Select*   This is an overnight broadcasting service. It transmits sponsored programmes which can be seen and recorded normally by anyone with a TV set. Programmes are also broadcast to subscribers who have BBC Selector equipment and this automatically scrambles and decodes them for viewing next day. BBC Select offers professional, educational and training programmes, and programmes to meet consumer interests.
- *Compact Disk Interactive (CD-I)*   Using a 'mouse', a CD-I player and a TV set or PC, you can explore a programme of still and moving pictures, sound, text and graphics on any subject a disk publisher thinks it worthwhile to market. This is multi-media and it offers exciting new ways of learning. Disks are made available with many language tracks so international barriers need not exist. The self-teaching prospects are numberless as are those for public relations, from multinational corporate training to many forms of sponsorship.

PERSONAL DIARY

It can go wrong

In 1993, to celebrate its 25th anniversary, *Hollis Press & Public Relations Annual* ran a competition asking readers of the IPR's journal to send in the funniest reminiscences of their public relations careers. Part of Ian Houston's winning entry read:

My first real PR job was to publicise a new fibreglass boat, featuring built-in buoyancy: the Unsinkable Dory stays afloat even when full of water. Not a bad story-line I thought, and set about organising a waterborne press demonstration, engaging photogenic models, and selecting glamorous photographs of boats.

I picked a day in the 'silly season' with no major news, checked weather forecasts, sent the invites, pre-sold the story to the press. The response was terrific. Several nationals said yes, and all the trade press were coming. Piece of cake I thought. But nemesis was at hand.

Demo day dawned, and the sun shone. We sped the press around Bedfont Lake, drinks in hand. The models modelled and the cameras clicked. Confidence grew as I extolled the virtues of 'this unsinkable boat'. Then some cynic from the *Express* picture desk said: 'Let's see how it does with the water in it then.' No problem, I thought, filling the bilges. The models got damp but their smiles didn't slip.

'What about some more people in? You said it's unsinkable.'

Abandoning caution, I crammed the boat with people and we motored out for another photo session with the hull almost full of water.

'Stand up and wave,' shouted a friendly photographer.

As we did, the Unsinkable Dory – by now completely water-logged and quite unstable – turned gracefully but inexorably over, propelling everyone into the water. I could hear the camera shutters slamming open even as I fell, and they were still going when I surfaced, dragging two half-drowned models back ashore.

As I bravely pointed out, the boat really was unsinkable; it was just floating upside down. But it was all futile, and the nationals loved it. I had just found out what makes news.

6.2 Print, paper and publications

You need to decide what job any publication has to do. What is it for? Who will read it? Will they read it? How to get them to read even some of it? Is there a better way of communicating with these particular publics? Or, like the report and accounts, are you obliged to produce it?

Print comes in all shapes and sizes but in most countries will be one of the international paper sizes, see Fig. 6.4. Sometimes you choose an odd size to catch attention but someone is bound to complain about the wastage of paper, the difficulty of finding envelopes and the increased cost of postage.

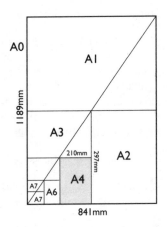

Fig. 6.4 Paper is cut to standard international sizes: series A for print and stationery, series B for posters and series C for envelopes. Each successively smaller sheet is created by halving the long side of the previous, larger sheet. The diagram shows the common A4 stationery size in the context of other sheets

Documents longer than four pages need to be bound (at the 'finishing' stage). The most common method for booklets – say up to 64 pages – is saddle stitching, where two staples are punched into the gutter.

The pages then stay open easily for reading. Other methods include comb binding and spiral wire binding, see Fig. 6.5.

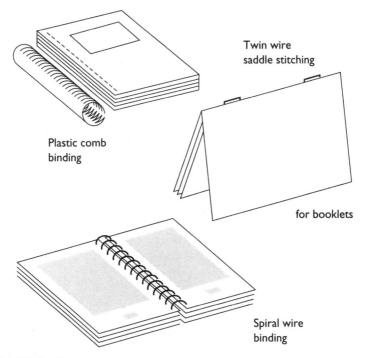

Twin wire
saddle stitching

Plastic comb
binding

for booklets

Spiral wire
binding

Fig. 6.5 Comb binding and spiral wire binding

Perfect binding is used for books, with the paper glued in sections at the spine. This is suitable for up to about 200 pages. Above this, stitched sections are needed.

Leaflets made out of one sheet only need folding. The Americans call them 'flyers'.

It is worth having a picture in your mind of the likely format because it helps in preparing the copy, the sequence of the layout, the way the illustrations are used. Single A4 sheets make simple newsletters, one or two-sided, simple leaflets, or can be designed on each of the six panels created by folding the A4 sheet to fit a DL envelope, see Fig. 6.6.

Printed on board weights (above 170gsm – grammes per square metre) such a leaflet can include a reply-paid card. The type, weight and shade

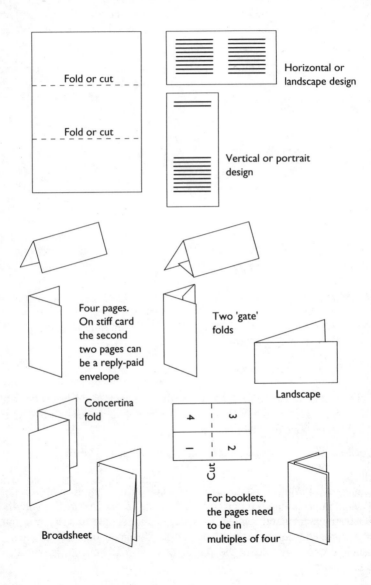

Fold or cut

Fold or cut

Horizontal or landscape design

Vertical or portrait design

Four pages. On stiff card the second two pages can be a reply-paid envelope

Two 'gate' folds

Landscape

Concertina fold

4   3

1   2

Cut

Broadsheet

For booklets, the pages need to be in multiples of four

Fig. 6.6 Some ways to fold leaflets

of paper makes a difference. Art (or gloss) is shiny; matt (or silk) is non-reflective. Cartridge is crisp but not particularly good for black-and-white half-tone reproduction of photographs, never mind full-colour photographs, whether from transparencies (best for reproduction) or colour prints.

Coloured paper can stand out in a mailing or add variety to a brochure or report and accounts but is not very good for photographs. While gloss papers look up-market, too much shine makes them hard to read; matt papers have a restrained quality but the pages get dirty more easily.

The weight of paper ranges from copier thickness (80 gsm) up to 350gsm (heavy cover board). Self-cover is when you use the same paper for the covers as for the pages. To have thicker covers you need at least eight pages inside, otherwise the brochure will promise much but look thin.

Papermakers have been working at improving the environmental soundness of their processes: what goes into the paper, the control of pollution, the conservation of energy. Many papers are now partly, or even wholly, made from recycled waste paper or no longer use chlorine for pulp bleaching. Don't believe the one about a heap of computer printouts representing so much chopped down rain forest. Whatever the past failings of the paper industry in environmental terms, paper is made from softwood trees grown for the purpose.

Don't forget that paper can be given a variety of embossed finishes to make it more interesting and stylish. Fashions come and go in the shade of paper – creamy coloured or bright white. Duller shades came in with the environmental pressures but bleaching without chlorine is now common and 'bluer' whites are popular again. Some companies and designers like the texture of uncoated recycled paper, making a virtue of its roughness and poorer colour reproduction.

All these physical considerations should be at the back of your mind when planning publications and are worth discussing with the publication's designer and with a printer (to ensure there are no snags). One can affect the other. Make friends with one or two printers so that you can keep up with the developments in technology and have someone you can ask for a quick price on how much a publication will cost.

The main factors which dictate price are the length of the print run (5000 copies or 250,000), the number of pages, whether there are photographs, the number of colours to be run, the type of paper used and the charging practices of the printer.

Most corporate print uses colour (called process colour or 4-colour). The photographs are produced using just four (process) colours: yellow, cyan (process blue), magenta and black. Each colour is printed as a fine set of dots at a different angle to each other and slightly offset from the other colours to make the classical rosette formation you can see under a magnifying glass. Technology is around which makes these much finer (therefore producing a sharper reproduction) and which involves eight dots instead of the traditional four. If you use process colour, which you have to if you want colour illustrations, the price will be more than if you stick to black-and-white pictures and, say, a second colour to brighten the pages up. Printing used to be done one colour at a time. Larger printers have 4- and 5-colour machines which print the colours in sequence, in one sweep, using quick drying inks and electronic control.

If your printer isn't eager for you to come and look around, it's probably because he wants you to think he has a 5-colour machine. As long as his costs are reasonably comparative and he is giving you good service, this makes little practical difference but he will probably be limited economically by length of run.

The fifth colour can be useful when you want to have your organisation's own house colour printed solid. That way it is more consistent than if it is made up out of the four-colour set, the more common approach. A u/v (ultra violet) varnish can also be applied using the fifth colour facility. This is sometimes used to give an expensive-looking, slightly-raised, liquid shine appearance over the photographs of some corporate brochures.

It is worth acquiring a book of Pantone ink colours if you have much to do with publications. There are hundreds of ink colours made up by using different proportions of the constituent inks. Colours are always specified by the Pantone reference and it is essential that the printer takes notice of which is to be used. It is notoriously hard to keep a corporate colour consistent, not only because ink dries a different shade on different paper surfaces (offset paper absorbs more ink than a high gloss) but because the ink mixing may vary over a print run.

If you can obtain one of the books which show the effect of different tints (percentages of dots) of a colour when combined with another (80% yellow, 20% black) you are probably a good negotiator. They are expensive and elusive but at least go through one with a printer: the visual effects achieved are stimulating when you want to be sure how a colour panel will look. Nowadays you can see these effects on the computer screen before the disk is sent to the printer but the colours may not exactly match the printed result.

Bulletins

Daily or weekly bulletins are easy to produce using word processors or desk top publishing (dtp). You can set up a standard format, using simple typography, print off a copy direct from the printer and photo-copy the quantity you need to send out. You can include illustrations and photographs scanned into your system. You don't have to use digital methods. You can still paste copies of photographs (either screened on the photocopier or copied direct from the continuous-tone photograph) onto a laser print-out before photocopying. An approach like this can be useful for the covering sheet to photocopies of press cuttings being circulated as well as simple news and information bulletins.

With LAN (Local Area Networks) and WAN (Wide Area Networks) messaging systems where computer terminals are linked up internally and externally, simple bulletins can be distributed electronically – across the world in 10 seconds or so.

As photocopiers improve technologically, the scope for simple, immedi-ate communication of this kind will be enormous. Photocopiers with an editing board and stylus allow you to change originals electronically and reorganise them seamlessly. You can then print off what you want. In large companies you will configure your bulletins at your desk and transfer them electronically for printing on a central copier. Because digital networks are unifying, the previously separate functions of photocopying, laser printing and scanning can be combined.

Simple newsletters

It is a mistake to think because PCs make it easy for almost anyone to produce typeset documents, that the designer's skill and eye is no longer needed. It may be impracticable to have a designer lay out each issue of a simple newsletter, but at least have the style set profession-ally – and follow it. The designer's feeling for space, what is current in design, which typefaces go best together, colour and composition, are worth paying for.

Gather together typical contents, write a brief and have a style worked out professionally. You need a masthead (the arrangement of the title for your newsletter). The publication date and a subsidiary line of text explaining who the newsletter represents should appear in relation to it. Show the designer the length of story likely to appear. If articles are long you will not want four or five narrow columns because they will be too difficult to read and wasteful of space. Long lines of type are also difficult to read and inflexible in layout, so the page should be divided into two, three or four columns, with thought given to the size of the margins and the gutter between the columns of type. Tend to keep the same column arrangement on short newsletters but when there are eight pages or more, some contrast is welcome. Boxed panels can be used to the column widths, but then the words need setting to a narrower measure inside the box.

Notice that the width of the columns generally controls the size of illustrations. Four columns are a good choice for several short pieces and a largish picture. Two columns are rather rigid and unyielding, more suitable when you have longish articles which can be punctuated by a picture or two. Three columns are the popular choice for newsletters, offering variety and reasonably-sized photographs. If your newsletter carries advertising you will need to work out special sizes as there is no natural quarter-page size with three columns. Think about the margins. They can add relieving space and lead to less conventional column treatment. The margin space can be used to create interest by having small illustrations there or quotes from the text.

One of the reasons for choosing non-standard sizes of paper is the greater scope for column arrangement. The argument against is sometimes the practical one of envelope size and postage.

Type is easiest to read when justified left and right (making a straight vertical line on both sides of the column). Raggy right, or unjustified, is when the text is uneven on the right. This is softer in appearance, makes a change and can identify a separate item, especially if set in bold or italic.

For easy reading choose 'book' typefaces (with serifs, like the text of this book) rather than sans faces (like those used for the case studies in this book) which do not help the eye to read on in long sections of text. Sans faces can be used for headlines, or small, selected features (again, to provide contrast). The use of sans serif faces like Helvetica for classified advertising pages is based on there being many separate items which are not going to be read consecutively.

You should collect a few newsletters, study them, and model yours on approaches you like in relation to your audience.

Try to avoid allowing the software to design for you. And don't use printed effects just because they are easy to produce on the computer. One example is the fading tint, starting near 80 per cent solid and lightening down to 20 per cent and less. The result merely says: 'designed by computer'.

Simply produced, but professionally written and laid-out, newsletters are cheap yet so flexible it is a puzzle they are not used more for keeping in touch with PR publics. They do not even need much news. Views, issues, photographs, reminders, useful information, testimonials and cartoons are just as relevant for many audiences. Any organisation with a standard mailing list can usefully send out a newsletter with a reply-paid card once or twice a year. It's a ready-made insert for magazines, a 'stuffer' to send out with general correspondence, a response item, background information.

Corporate literature

Although you will want considerable variation between publications – different content will dictate that anyway – you also need the harmony of an instantly identifiable source. This is where a corporate style has power.

Specialist publications   Print offers a wide field for sponsoring the publication of specialist journals, books or periodicals in sectors which tie in with an organisation's objectives. Even small companies can benefit through a trade-off. For instance, paper merchants Classic Papers have co-operated with colleges of design by supplying free paper in return for a run-on of a publication showing students' work – the printed images show the quality of the paper.

The organisation's logo or symbol should be a repetitive companion. The colours of the livery should be used as part of the design. Have one or two typefaces that are regularly used, leaflet to leaflet, brochure to brochure. It isn't wise to be too hidebound in this because individual occasions will arise when something different will work better. But if all the organisation's print has a common look about it, awareness is increased and a feeling for the corporate style developed. This should not be too stark, or uncompromising, or heavy-handed, otherwise that is the impression received. The best corporate styles allow plenty of variation and deviation while the source is still clearly identifiable.

One of the cleverest corporate identities was created in the 1960s when Wolff Olins designed the humming bird with the Bovis logo, against a spacey white background. It has: variation, the different positions of the bird; wit, because of these postures; clarity, in the simple, solid company name. The four-colour rendering of the bird might have been expensive for some applications but the impact more than compensates.

The ultimate piece of print is the corporate brochure. Much money is spent on this and much is wasted. Sometimes they seem like a pat way of giving out information without really telling you much or taking too much individual trouble. Sometimes they don't seem intended to be read but, rather, held, page-turned, admired. If they evoke a feeling of a job well done, of an organisation of substance, they will have achieved their aim.

Electronic developments

- *ISDN*

    Fibre-optic telephone line technology has created the Integrated Services Digital Network (ISDN). For those with a modem link on their telephone system this carries digitised computer data at high speed – everything from video-conferencing to Prestel.

    The effect on print preparation has been dramatic. The pages of any publication – text, pictures, graphics, colour, tints – can be sent backwards and forwards electronically for proofing and correction on screen, from one desk top publishing PC system to another wherever they may be, in another office, town or country.

    Text and layout can be altered at one end or the other and photographs cropped differently on screen while you watch and agree. With the appropriate equipment all illustrations can be scanned into the computer, including colour photographs. Film for the printer is then produced in the four-colour separations either on the spot or by passing the information, stored on a disk, to an output bureau. The halfway house is to produce film for text and simple tint but to have colour photograph separations made independently and stripped into the film by the printer.

- *On-line publishing*

    The growth of Internet, the worldwide link-up of PCs and data bases, has turned E-mail into a paperless publishing outlet. Electronic newsletters, journals and magazines are becoming known as e-zines.

    By taking part in the Internet you can make your publication avail able to anyone who sends a message for it to be down-loaded to their E-mail box. World Wide Web does the same for hypertext so that multi-media on-line magazines can be electronically transferred complete with sound and pictures.

Targeting may be a problem but it will be interesting to study the Net as a communications medium from the public relations standpoint. So far it is essentially a free-wheeling, anarchic world of some 40 million subscribers in which people attempting to use it for advertising have been 'flamed' (metaphorically scorched by vitriolic E-mail protests).

- *Databases*

  It remains to be seen how far the ability of the individual to call up information, through PC and modem, will reduce the role of the journalist as interpreter of information.

6.3   Audio-visual presentations

You can speak to people, write things down for them or show them pictures, still or moving. There are skills to be learned for each.

Today's world is strongly audio-visual. Familiarity with television means that people are used to listening to words (however garbled) and watching moving pictures (which takes time), rather than making an effort to dig information out of the written word. Symptomatic are the half-page summaries in national newspapers of the main stories covered. The most commonly quoted statistic about words and pictures is that you are likely to remember 60 per cent of the message that uses both together, perhaps only 20 per cent using either on their own. Although, for how long? For good or ill, today's world is one of impressions rather than information. There is too much so-called information about for it to be remembered for long or stored for easy recall.

Working in public relations you need a good knowledge of visual ways of communicating. This ranges from the impression given by an organis-ation's graphic style (or corporate identity, in management-speak), understanding statistics presented in pie charts and bar graphs, and knowing about the world of artists and designers in general, through to 35mm slides, acetates for overhead projection, slide-tape presen-tations, video, film and computer-generated visuals.

Your knowledge will come to be in two parts: things you can do to some extent yourself, and those you rely on specialists to do for you.

You should aim to know enough about visual communication not to be overcharged by a specialist, and to be able to contribute constructively. Above all, you should equip yourself to stay in control of what is happening, while allowing creativity and expertise full rein. You will need, at one time or another, to make presentations and to help colleagues and clients to do so. This immediately raises the question of visual aids. Whether it is a pitch for new business, a press conference, a new product launch or communicating with employees, you will have to decide how to present information persuasively.

Free-standing displays

As a background you might have a portable display set up carrying words and photographs, and examples of print. The photographs, and other visuals, could be dry-mounted on card. Many such display stands are available. The display boards might be made as a unit fitting into the frame, or separately-mounted illustrations could be fastened by Velcro. In your early days in PR you might find yourself with the task of helping to locate, design, erect and dismantle such a portable display as a background setting for a press conference, hospitality tent or hotel room exhibition. It can be combined: with a repeating video, with electronic headline units that ripple digital letters along in news flash fashion; with a computer-generated display; or with moving displays.

35mm slide shows

Many topics (such as travel, leisure, architecture and fashion) are highly photogenic. Cameras now have automatic light sensing and focusing so it is easy to take your own 35mm transparencies. One of the easiest types of presentation, therefore, is a well-ordered collection of slides using a carousel projector. Be handy with a camera and take one with you wherever you may come across pictures relevant to a topic you may have to talk on. Or encourage your client to. Many opportunities for photographing the installation of engineering equipment, for instance, are lost because no one carries a camera. (They are just as useful for a brochure or a newsletter as for a slide show.)

You can have slides made from computer-generated images to mix with your shots or borrow slides from a photo-library (but don't lose them: it can be expensive).

Slide shows may smack of holiday snaps, but they have many advantages.

- The slides become your prompt. You can talk with little need of notes; just look at the picture and it will remind you of what you want to say
- Slides suit any size of audience, from a few people in a partially darkened room to a conference auditorium with all the professional gear
- The remote control, once you have tried it out, is a pain-free, professional way of moving the slide on. You do not want to be nodding to an assistant who then gets the slides out of sync with what you are saying
- You can seal fixed sequences of slides into labelled trays for frequently-given talks, or make several copies of the same talk. You can pick the slides you want from a store and slot them into a carousel, then build what you say around them. Number them in case of accident
- The quality of the image on the screen is much better than with overhead projection acetates.

Don't forget to put glass covers on the cardboard mounts to protect the transparency from the heat of the projector. Your organisation can buy special cabinets to store slides. When there is no space, unmounted film can be kept in stamp album pockets and mounted temporarily for the show.

Overhead projection (O/H)

This is a method of presentation which has been unfairly maligned by those who think professionalism means showing a video. Overhead projection is common in teaching settings when presentation matters less than getting across information clearly.

Like anything else, it needs thinking out and rehearsing but it is infinitely flexible in regard to content and time constraints, and is highly personal in terms of presentation. It is not 'slick' – but who wants that all the time? – and allows more of your character to come across. It connects you closely to your audience because you are constantly changing the visuals, selecting which ones to show next. It is also effective in question and answer sessions.

An overhead projector is, in effect, a light box with a mirror on an arm above it to reflect the image on your acetate onto a screen (or blank white wall) behind you. Each image is on an A4 sheet of acetate which you place, face up, on the light box when you wish to show it on the screen. The images can be words, diagrams, sketches, photographs.

You can draw or write on the acetate with special, coloured fibre-tipped pens. You can have diagrams prepared on disk and printed out directly onto the A4 acetate sheets, or colour photocopied onto them.

Whatever you do, only use heat-treated acetate sold for the purpose. If you have run out of acetates don't think you can cut up a plastic folder as a substitute to save the day: the photocopier will self-destruct.

For someone who is not a naturally good, or highly trained, presenter, overheads offer great scope. They concentrate the audience on the information being given rather than on the superficial smoothness of a performance.

You can use O/H in many ways.

- Put a list on the acetate and start with it covered up by a sheet of paper which you gradually move down to reveal successive points. This is the equivalent of build-up slides on 35mm when information is added slide by slide with the current point highlighted in a different colour
- Overlay acetates one on another to build up information on the screen
- Mask the acetate and cut hinged windows in the mask so that they can be opened to reveal a set of connected information or illustration
- Write on the acetate while it is on the light box
- Use a ruler, stick or pen (but preferably not your finger) to point out something on the acetate – its shadow points on the screen.

The acetates can be kept loose in the right order, in pockets in a ring binder or in cardboard frames (which make them bulkier for transit but you can write your speaker's notes on them in the same way as preparing a flip chart lightly in pencil). If you want to sit down for some of the presentation, make up a ring binder of photocopies of your acetates, again with full notes written on, and keep that in front of you. Be sure all messages on your acetates are large and clear. Do not have too many words to a sheet.

Small-scale presentations

When talking to one person or just a few, you can convert 35mm slides or A4 acetate information to paper and put them in A3 sales presenters. The pages can be flipped over at close quarters with less ceremony than on the big stage of screen projection. Or you can have them out and show them separately. Mount them on card and prop them up on an easel or flip chart.

Presentations can be kept on disk for use on PCs and a computer screen presentation for two or three people gathered round.

Slide-tape programmes

These combine sound, music and slides and, looking like a small television set, can be carried around. If two projectors are used slides can be made to dissolve into each other and then the images are usually projected across the room.

Multi-image presentations

These are the shows you see on holiday at historical sites, varying in quality in accordance with the technology at the time they were created. You sit in a small theatre and watch several images at a time. Technically multi-image begins at three or more projectors and can go on to ten or more. This all increases the visual tricks that can be played and it sometimes takes an effort to remember that you are seeing still, not moving, images, so fast may they be juxtaposed.

Multi-screen is different in that more screens are used, often for panoramic effects with several 35mm slides. It is still multi-screen if several areas of one screen are used for projecting different images.

Videowalls

For the moment, the ultimate in multi-screen and multi-image combined is the videowall, those banks of television-like screens. These can show one huge, if criss-crossed, image, or many smaller ones simultaneously – or both. These are in action at centres like the Museum of the Moving Image in London or the automobile museum in Nevada. The technology is used in concourses (airports, railway stations, malls), at exhibitions, indoor arenas and visitor centres. Small videowall banks now appear in shops and the reception areas of big companies. The Wellcome Trust, for instance, has what it calls an 'electronic tapestry' in the foyer of the Wellcome Building.

Computer-controlled projection

Sophisticated presentations can be given using the PC or multi-media as the source for visuals and linking them electronically to larger screens that can be seen easily by the audience.

Videos

Every organisation needs a corporate video. Not. At least, a lot of consideration should be given before jumping in. Everyone tends to accept videos as a necessary part of the communication process. But they can be seriously counterproductive: if they are amateurly produced; if they are blatantly commercial or ultra-corporate in language ('We at Zonx Technological Inc are the leading edge of the customer service interface'); if they are shallow; or too long. The larger the organisation the more video is a likely choice sooner or later. At costs of at least £6000 upwards (over £1000 a minute) and very often £50,000 or more, they can eat up budget.

Videos are not the choice if you are trying to convey a stream of detailed, factual information which you wish the audience to remember. On the other hand, videos have external uses in selling, at exhibitions, on roadshows, at conferences and setting the scene about an organisation when you first walk in. They can help reassure shareholders, and stakeholders such as customers and employees; explain about problems and issues; influence people's judgements, attitudes and behaviour. Internally, they can aid communication with employees in a human, realistic, interesting way. In far-flung organisations, they enable directors and managers to talk to employees with whom there would otherwise be no contact (even if this isn't always two-way communication). The annual financial results can be presented by the CEO or finance director. Information about product lines can be given (video is good for showing, for demonstration). The latest merger talks, the mission, values, reorganisation in the face of change, redundancies – all are subjects where video can help understanding.

People are more used to watching television these days than reading, which makes video a familiar medium. So some organisations produce an occasional video news magazine for staff to see. This medium might also be chosen to record an event which is important to an organisation; an anniversary is the most obvious.

Before you start thinking about how to make a video, work out how it will be shown. A press release is wasted if it is sent to the wrong place, or late. How much more costly to invest heavily in a video – and you can hardly do just the one – which has little chance of being viewed. How, when, where is it going to be seen? In small groups, a theatre, the canteen, at home or what? It isn't really sufficient anyway just to show a video: you need to brief local management, arrange for an introduction and explanation and for questions to be answered, produce a reminder pack for viewers to take away. (How much do you retain of what you see for long without a prompt?) You have to think about the problem of language if the video is to be shown overseas. And is the format compatible with the equipment it will be shown on? Is there any equipment? Finally, you need to arrange for feedback – what did they think, how better to do it next time?

Back to the beginning. Why make a video in the first place? Who will make up the audience? What are they to learn from the video? What pattern of presentation to use: professional presenter (for a fee), voice-over, interviews, mere 'talking heads', documentary footage? Should there be a script (which must be how people talk not how they write) or a general bullet point guide? What are the audience to learn from the video?

THE BRIEF

Why is the programme being made?
Who is the target audience?
What do you want to communicate?
What do you want the audience to do?
How do you want the message put across?
Where and how will the programme be shown?
When is it needed?
What will it cost?
Who will be the principal point of contact?
What else do they need to know?

From *Commissioning a programme* published by the International Visual Communications Association (IVCA).

Now it's time to consult a video production company, brief them – aims, content, timings, budget – and keep closely in touch with them. Your budget should cover copying the video, creating the print support package to accompany it, and any new presentation equipment needed. Organise a clear-cut sequence of management approval to agree: your brief; the initial treatment proposals from the production company; the script; first and second editing stages; who is to take part; locations.

Video-making has plenty of scope for flashing a knowledge of technical terms. A Noddie is a cut-a-way of people reacting to a discussion on camera; Chromakey is replacing one image with another on an area of colour; a BCU is (of course) a Big Close-Up; call and wrap time is when a sequence of filming starts and finishes.

Leave the making of the video to the video company. Concentrate on looking after the interests of your employer by checking that the budget covers all pre-production, production, post-production needs and all expenses. Smooth the way for the video team to operate on company locations. Keep a close eye on the progress of the first headline script outline and the shooting script the video will use. Confirm in writing the procedure for approving extra costs, who owns the legal rights, liability in case of accident, theft or damage to equipment, insurance and timings. Learn how employees need to dress and present themselves for filming. If there is casting for actors' parts, be present. Check that communication with employee actors is efficient – normally done through a call sheet.

Expect a pre-production team of three or four, performing between them the roles of producer, director, writer, production manager and secretary. A director and producer will handle production, with a filming crew of two or three. Post-production includes hiring an editing suite. For off-line (the roughcut) allow at least a day for every five minutes of the video. For on-line (the final edit that uses the rushes – video tapes – to make the finished master) allow an hour for every minute of the finished video.

Become knowledgeable about how people come across in front of the camera. You will have tried to insist on presentation training for management – an automatic response these days from public relations advisers when interviewers are about. You should obtain training for yourself. People are usually more natural when replying to a question and looking slightly off-screen at an interviewer (who may or may not be in the picture). Try to make sure they know what they are going to be asked and how long they will be 'on'. They should not memorise their responses but simply be aware of the main points.

Refer back to the original brief you drew up – it is your measure of how well the production is going.

The IVCA (International Visual Communication Association) runs an annual festival of film and video communications. The categories are: business and commercial training; technical training; education; recruitment; sales; retail marketing; corporate image; public relations; internal communications; science and technology; medical, public welfare; interactive; video publishing. The winner of the 1994 IVCA award public relations category was the University of Glasgow. Its video, Celebrating Science, was aimed at five publics: corporate business people, university staff and funding bodies, the general public, and potential 'scientists' uninspired by their school curriculum. Its aims, in celebration of the Century of Science at the university, were twofold. 'To promote the modern and 'user-friendly' image of the world of science to the public in general and to encourage more students to study and value science. To provoke discussion about wider issues regarding the potential of science, through its applications in commercial and industrial sectors, to solve many of the world's crucial problems.'

6.4 Sponsorship

These are days of partnerships, networking and good citizenship. Sponsorship fits naturally with each and is the ultimate you-scratch-my-back-and-I'll-scratch-your's enterprise. The principle is simple: one organisation pays for all or part of another's special activity costs in return for benefits in kind: mentions, tickets, promotional opportunities of various sorts. With the growth of satellite and cable television, the phenomenon of sponsorship is a common sight: 'this programme is brought to you by'; a tennis player wears a logo of a specific size; a racing car is in the sponsor's corporate colours; 'Cable and Wireless' printed on the stumps in the West Indies v England cricket matches (cricket match sponsors are now allowed a promotional patch of grass behind the bowler's run-up). Satellite television offers multi-nationals the ideal outlet, and one not beset by language problems.

Sponsorship is equally creative and useful on the smaller scale. In public relations terms, if the right activity can be identified, it offers an active, interesting, associative, cost-effective way to reach individual publics. This is just as valid for small companies as for large. Just to sponsor the menu for a dinner attended by leaders of your prime publics is to put your organisation's name in front of people who are important to you. So is offering a trophy; or providing relevant products on someone's stand at an exhibition; or funding a student scholarship or a local lecture. Just as long as it fits with the company's business aims, and people notice. And that is up to you, in the deal you make and the effort you put into possibilities for promotional ideas intrinsic to the sponsorship. All you have to decide is what your company can sponsor that will reach customers, prospects and publics economically.

While sponsorship is used as a marketing and selling tool, it is essentially public relations in its broad context. It is limited in the way it can inform a public and is more geared to persuasion by association of ideas. The character and style of the sponsored activity become associated with those of the sponsoring company. In the launch of a new product this association of one with the other adds value the longer it lasts, conditions public acceptance. If a company associates itself through sponsorship with something thought to be good, this moves it, in the public estimation, away from being yet another company without any social conscience out to make money.

This sense of association can extend to the use of brand colours being recognised on the product itself, without the brand name being known. The use of the company logo and livery colours is central to corporate image and reputation in promoting public awareness. Media coverage, a general target of public relations, is given a thorough boost by a sponsorship, not only in the launch announcement but continuously as the sponsorship unfolds. It is an ever-present 'peg' for stories as well as promotional opportunities. Sponsorship builds goodwill, provides ways of entertaining customers and distributors, adds to hospitality networking. It can even help recruitment by attracting more able people to the company.

Those who argue that public relations is not part of marketing but is the umbrella activity that stretches well beyond marketing, recognise the idea that PR helps create a more favourable trading climate. This is a function of sponsorship too. Stepping out ahead of a product campaign in a geographical area new to the sales force, sponsorship prepares the way. Identifying with a specific activity known for, say, its maleness or femininity or toughness or sense of good taste and culture, sponsorship forms conduits for transferring some of the chosen attributes to the sponsor. Such a link can add zest to a sale organisation.

Public relations activities are needed to make the sponsorship work, to get the most out of it. On the large scale it is television coverage – sight-lines and references – that count (and are counted). The legibility of the logo, the impact of company colours, the mentions agreed in the contract, the positioning of hoardings and banners, all need attending to. Employees must be kept informed and involved, thus opening up motivation schemes based on the sponsorship theme. Back-up print, newsletters, merchandising, photo-opportunities, related events, newspaper competitions, on-pack offers, point of sale advertising, film and video records – all are examples of activities which can be developed around the sponsorship. Even crisis PR comes into it: what happens if it rains, or there's a crash, or protestors don't like what's being sponsored?

Most sponsorship is for sporting events. The arts offer fewer opportunities, but gain from the cultural association businesses enjoy. Other areas for sponsorship are books, awards, education, exhibitions and expeditions. Appropriateness is always the key.

Sir Ranulph Fiennes felt his sponsorship by Damart thermal clothing to be ideal for his Siberian expedition because of the unity of the two. Other sponsorship choices have not matched so well, making it hard for the sponsor to recoup his outlay in terms of the media coverage he wants. Unlike Nigel Mansell, Sir Ranulph points out he is not 'splattered with names'. There is an extremely serious side to sponsorship, especially where manufacturers give equipment to be tried out under harsh conditions. 'Our lives,' says Sir Ranulph, 'are in the hands of the equipment manufacturers. The equipment must work at 40 degrees below. It can't just be a salesman's say so.'

Anything associated with the environment provides potential in the ozone-holed, pollution-threatened 1990s. Charities and voluntary organisations are ever more desperate for help as they find themselves competing for private funds.

Within reason, the longer the duration of the sponsorship, the better. A one-off, short-lived event (unless on the grand scale like the 1994 World Cup in America) does not give the same opportunities as one lasting several months. Hence the interest in league sports. If you have vigorous PR resources within your company, offer them in support of the mutual objective. While there must be some give and take in any sponsorship agreement, be sure the contract is firm about as much as possible. The list includes:

- Title
- Number of events
- Locations
- Corporate colours in the decor
- Personality appearances
- Extended PR
- Use of the sponsored product
- Free tickets
- References to the sponsor (over a public address system, for instance)
- Your use of events for your own promotional displays
- Television coverage.

Sole sponsorship gives you the best chance of making waves but of course it costs more and can harm your company's reputation if something goes badly wrong or you have chosen an unfortunate liaison. Primary sponsors share with others; sometimes one or two main sponsors take equal credit but more usually they will join with secondary sponsors who have only a specialised interest, say as official suppliers for a product. Taking over sponsorship from a company now well associated with an activity has special PR problems because of the inevitably lingering presence of the previous company.

Impartiality is a quality of editorial coverage which is missing from advertising. The opportunity to be covered in the press as part of day-to-day events is attractive to companies. But be aware that journalists are not employed to mention your product. Indeed research suggests that they still make independent judgements and will not submit to the railery of frustrated sponsors. Building the company or brand name tightly and crisply into the title of the event is the best tactic. Mentioning it in this context is more natural and acceptable for a journalist. Some sponsorship credits could be so long there would be no room for the story. Sometimes sponsorship *is* the story. In any case, you should not be seeking to overwhelm the media with blatant plugs – whether TV, radio or press. They are not the point; the activity itself is, and people will switch off if you overdo it. That said, the media are much more conscious nowadays of needing to encourage the private sector when that helps to keep activities alive that would otherwise die. The theatre, for one, is badly in need of such support.

One of the benefits of the new PR courses for students is that they stimulate research as the basis of dissertations. Rachel Truett, who studied at the College of St Mark and St John, looked into the credits given by journalists to sponsors. Sports and arts correspondents would generally co-operate if the sponsor's name was part of the title, of interest to readers or there was space available. Holding a press event would certainly not produce a credit, but a threat of closure might. Rachel quoted many arts and sports editors' views. For example: 'Without sponsorship for the arts we won't get events, and newspapers should do their bit' (Christopher Hansford, *Bath Evening Chronicle*); and 'A sponsor would be credited when they're the only sponsor, it's a major show and it can be done without disturbing the flow of the article' (Tim De Lisle, *Independent on Sunday*). Sports editors: '. . . we do not see ourselves as a begging bowl or recruitment agency for events looking for sponsorship' (Tom Clarke, *The Times*); 'Our job is simply to report on events, not give free advertising. Equally however, we don't deliberately not include sponsors' names' (Ian Passingham, *Colchester Evening Gazette*).

Media sponsorship

Recession makes newspapers less choosy when a deal can be struck for sponsoring part of the paper. Some steer away from it, others may look for sponsorship of a page, a column, a crossword. *The European* will even publish a special edition carrying a company logo for use at special events. The most popular vehicle is a supplement because it is by definition extra to the paper's normal, independent reporting and feature writing. The advertisement feature (so headed) is an ad in editorial form. The 'advertorial' is more sophisticated, with a core of independently written editorial surrounded by support advertising from many competitive sources. The 'sponsorial' goes even further, often featuring one company with by-lined editorial independently written by staff journalists, although clearly branded with the sponsor's logo, forming a pull-out supplement.

An example is when Digital Equipment Corporation linked up with the *Sunday Times* in 1993 over a 16-page supplement: Back to the Black – A Guide to Improving Business Performance. This carried Digital advertising and a competition but was written independently by *Sunday Times* journalists (who mentioned competitors); the supplement also carried competitors' advertising. Readership of the supplement was encouraged by a front-page reference to an Institute of Management survey which was picked up on in the supplement. This was not surprising, as it was commissioned for Digital by their PR consultancy Biss Lancaster, who had conceived the supplement idea to convey the spread of Digital's business operations.

Journalists have always distanced themselves from their advertisement departments. That doesn't stop the ad people being a good source of information on forthcoming editorial features, unlisted as well as listed. Some trade editors will not deny a connection between the amount of advertising placed and the appearance of editorial matter. Sometimes, as with the colour separation problem, the media seems more anxious in small ways to 'corrupt' itself than PR people are. (The ethics of a company paying for the costs of producing a colour photograph to illustrate editorial in a trade journal, without the fact being stated on the page, are still being debated.)

Programme sponsorship

The ITC regulations were changed in 1990 to allow programme sponsorship. Pamela Atack wrote her student dissertation on the topic in 1993 and found, from interviews with sponsors, that the same principles, of long-term association rather than short-term selling tactics, apply here. Full exploitation of off-air opportunities is essential: launching to the media, developing back-up material, arranging events. PowerGen, sponsoring the weather forecast, produced videos and teaching packs for schools. Swatch watches identified themselves with the programme The Word to convey their 'provocative joy of life', and to reflect the innovative nature of the company. Konica sponsored a holiday snaps programme and were able to carry over the link to their advertising by using the same jingle.

6.5 Exhibitions

Exciting. Messy. Depressing. Tiring. Full of opportunities.

As a manager you are bound to be involved sooner or later with an exhibition your organisation is taking part in. You may be questioning the wisdom and cost of it, enjoying the sales benefits, speaking at the associated conference, helping organise the stand or driving across Europe at the last minute with crucial material in the boot of your car. As a newcomer to the PR department you may be one of the people your colleagues turn to for help.

For anyone interested in PR, visiting a few shows such as the Ideal Home to see how exhibitors are presenting themselves to customers is worthwhile. You will learn a lot about what's good and what's bad in selling, marketing, public relations and the quality of products in that business sector. If you are helping with a stand, make sure you are the one taking the press releases or press packs to the press office. And hang around to have a look at how the information is presented. Some do it well but so often it is a last minute thing.

Exhibitions are an ideal training ground for anyone intent on a career in public relations or the associated disciplines. In the first place, taking part is a specific business and management decision which means evaluating the right exhibition, thorough research, budget considerations and costs (all of them), logistics, time. It can be one of the most comprehensive mental exercises open to you and one that touches many parts of the organisation. It may be an early introduction to travelling abroad on business.

The temptation is strong to go into an exhibition. Perhaps 'to fly the flag' or because the competition is there. Or for what might be called PR reasons: to project the company's image. As taking part can be expensive in terms of all the paraphernalia needed, *'why* are we exhibiting?' is the question. However, once the decision has been taken – which will depend on the relevance of the potential visitors to your product or service, and what you will get out of it in relation to what it costs you, and how better you could spend the time and money – then public relations becomes paramount.

Suddenly, however much the exhibition is about selling, it is equally about public relations:

- Now your reputation is at stake
- The exhibition must be used to build and reinforce corporate identity
- Public relations activities become an integral part of planning before, during and after the exhibition.

Read the small print of the organiser's manual; it's an experience. It is also essential for knowing what you can or cannot do. In the 1960s, when the trade unions were rampant in the UK exhibition world, you could trigger a strike by lifting a hammer. Nowadays you are most likely to be checking night-time security, how early you can arrive to set up; or whether you can have someone handing out leaflets around the halls. The manual also details the organiser's publicity arrangements for the exhibition. This is where your knowledge can shine: so many of the ordinary possibilities are overlooked or done inefficiently.

The organiser's publicity

Find out about how the organiser will promote the show. Pre-show leaflets could include your company's name, story or a photograph. Press releases sent out by the organisers could include interesting new information from you.

Help them with their publicity.

- Make the most use of your free entry in the exhibition catalogue
- Take advantage of the offer of stickers, posters, multi-lingual leaflets, complimentary tickets
- If there is to be an organised visit of overseas press, try to become involved
- Check what media the organisers will be alerting; many of them will represent your own prime targets
- Big companies can bargain with the organisers: if they are spending heavily on visitor promotion they often negotiate the *quid pro quo* of a discount on stand costs.

Your own publicity

Before the show   Your concern is to attract your prime customers and potential customers.

- Establish how the stand design can be themed to help. A strong theme could be a story in itself and help in the direct mail invitations
- Try to have an active demonstration taking place on the stand
- Bigger companies (who might be advertising anyway) will link their ads to the exhibition
- Attach stickers to correspondence
- Post special letters and invitations to your main business prospects
- Comb your trade press for preview opportunities by supplying a good article on an unusual aspect of your exhibit
- At the least, send press releases to all the journals which will preview the exhibition, in a precise form that needs little alteration (subbing). Try to provide them with good photographs, especially in colour. (The use of colour pictures is widespread now.)
- If you have an important innovation, see if you can provide a by-lined article to a trade journal just beforehand
- Mention that your company will be at the exhibition in all other media material you issue and in advertising. The exhibition is a peg upon which you can hang stories that might not otherwise be of interest
- Look out for picture and interview opportunities for local TV and radio.

During the show   Make sure the press office has a press kit from your company (even if it is only a plastic folder with a news release and a photograph). A company folder with the logo on the cover is smarter. Try to have a copy of the photograph displayed on the press office pinboard. The pack should give succinct information, preferably hard news, and direct journalists to your stand. Be a frequent visitor to the press office to check stocks (and to see your material hasn't got hidden), find out reactions, bump into journalists.

Have the same press kits available on the stand, and not just on press day; journalists can turn up at other times and, anyway, the press information can be handy to show visitors. Use the exhibition as the occasion to announce a noteworthy contract. Use it as the venue for a pre-arranged interview with one of your company's specialists. Most exhibitions will have an interview room. But make sure company technical specialists are primed and know what they are saying – you must be aware of the ground they will cover because of the consequences of saying 'the wrong thing' to the media.

See if you can think up a visually interesting happening – a stunt, a presentation, a celebrity visit, a demonstration. Exhibition stands can be boring photographically, so photographers will be glad of some activity. Put up notices in the press office to announce the time of the photo-opportunity (but give advance notice too). Even if you do not attract anyone, be sure to have your own photographer there and send out the story yourself.

Finding speaking opportunities for key managers is a common PR task (see the account executive's efforts in Chapter 7). You will have thought about this well beforehand – when you saw there was a conference, seminar, workshop or panel discussion tied in with the exhibition, and tried to arrange a slot for one of your 'experts'. You then have the text of what they say as possible editorial material on the day or, embargoed, earlier (to fit in with press deadlines). And another chance of a photograph.

The photography may easily be too plain and unevocative for the press but you still have a useful tool for your own newsletter or for a leaflet, or as file material. Try to be in the habit of having a camera and a small tape recorder with you at an exhibition. You never know, royalty may pass by unannounced or your technical director suddenly start explaining all sorts of things you don't know.

Sometimes companies book a room nearby for their own reception or party. Some even cheat and hold their own private exhibition in a nearby hotel room. Exhibitions are, above all, occasions for personal contact with people important to the company. You have to make the most of this throughout. It used to be called making contacts; now it's called networking.

Logistics   You may well become involved in the physical side of exhibition stands, not only the words and graphics but assembly. Plan well ahead. Consider how they are to be transported, and the weight and size of the display sections in relation to facilities at the venue.

6.6 Working with photographers and designers

Designers

Keeping control of, or at least in touch with, a project once it has been absorbed by a designer is an invaluable, and stressful, skill. If left to themselves, designers tend to take any project into their own special world. Most PR people are not *sympathique* with design, seeing it as just something 'the designer should come up with'.

If you work for a big company there is scope for employing the more expensive design consultants. Indeed, if you don't, and the design is disliked, you will be blamed for not using one of the big names. Large companies are called in for the layout of reports and accounts; spectacular corporate brochures; the new logo (even only slightly revised); and vehicle livery. It is as well to remember, too, that while design charges may be high, the cost of changing signs, lorries and stationery throughout an organisation will be considerably more.

Here you are working with design companies who recognise that design cannot be divorced from communication. So they add that word to their title. This allows them to add research into their portfolio (to find out what ideas the design should express).

If you work for a small company you should try hard to locate freelance designers, become familiar with their work, what they are good and bad at, what they are likely to charge, how quickly they can respond and on what scale. A combination of freelance designers and specialist illustrators can be fruitful. As long as you have the money, it pays for designers to be familiar with a project early on. Their ideas on format and presentation may take you somewhere you could not otherwise go. However, the further you can work up a simple project yourself, in terms of words, format and early rough visuals, the more control you will have.

Never put design work in hand without a written brief or confirmation of what is wanted. This may be a carefully worked out document or simply a memo detailing your needs. You should be specific about costs and timings. Be clear in your own mind of the steps involved. The traditional stages in design are: scamps (rough visuals of several broad approaches); layouts (showing how the design will look); type mark-up (specifying the faces to be used); artwork (which the printer will photograph to produce printing plates); proofs; and the final print run.

Today it can be hard work persuading the designer to do preliminary pencil or magic marker scamps. Many designers, having learnt the arts of Quark EXpress or Illustrator, seem to lose the desire to come back out of the computer.

The whole document can be proofed up as a colour visual, or passed down the line to your computer. No type mark-ups are needed. The artwork can be produced by the designer, the client, the repro house, or the printer. The creative and production processes are converging.

To become familiar with the way design and technology are progressing, read *Creative Technology* magazine. To learn how designers think, look at *Creative Review* from time to time. To find designers, talk to people you know in print and advertising. When you see design work you like, find out who did it. Keep looking, even when you have no immediate need.

Photography

Become familiar with the work, the way of working, and charges of several photographers. Find out what they are good at. Those working on papers, at local or national level, can be worth getting to know.

There are several recurring circumstances for which you need to be photographically prepared:

- People receiving awards
- Speakers at seminars, press conferences, the AGM
- Visitors to offices and factories
- Photo-calls (when you need your own pictures, whoever turns up from the media)
- Product shots in the studio and on site
- Pictures for newsletters, house magazines (it can be worth becoming photo-literate yourself if there is no reasonable budget for a photographer)
- Mugshots of management for appointment releases.

Speed of processing photographs is important. Many shots, to be any use, must meet press deadlines for tomorrow's paper, Friday's local weekly, next month's technical or trade journal. These deadlines often govern when you take pictures, and certainly how they are sent (courier, wire, first-class post). Photo agencies are the best bet if you need same-day service.

There will usually be more time for photographs for corporate brochures and product leaflets. Best, however, to get on with it. Although photographers take pictures in an instant, they can take days to deliver the results. Always allow plenty of time, even for ordinary shots, especially if the photographer is bringing his own lighting. Insist, politely, on looking down the camera viewfinder, to check the shot. Some photographers do not like it, but how otherwise can you know what you are paying for unless they take trial shots with an instant print camera?

Colour or black and white? Colour transparency or colour print? How many are needed. Give it thought; the photographer needs to know. Find out as much as you can about the site in advance, and tell the photographer; it may affect what equipment he brings. Transparencies are best for colour reproduction; colour negative film is best for direct colour prints, say for an exhibition. Colour transparencies can be printed in black and white. They can be copied, too, but at £7–10 a time, sending out 20 to journals for their colour pages can use up a budget fairly quickly. On occasions when the subject is static, have the same shot taken a couple of dozen times.

For the kind of photograph that might make a national, you will need help. If you have what you think could be a photo-story, talk to the picture editor of the most appropriate newspaper about the possibility of an exclusive or to a photographer well-versed in such work. With the coming of colour to newspapers, it can be worth contacting the picture editor if you have an imaginative, unusual photograph of an event, or the idea for one. A good picture can be front-page news in itself.

7

—— A CAREER IN PR ——

7.1 Getting started

You need a certain degree of personal resilience to do public relations. It is a career, ironically, which has always had a fight for its own image and reputation. Although you know that what you do is a good, honest job for your employer or client, someone always denigrates public relations with some gratuitous insult. An interviewer on the Today Programme asked: 'Is that just public relations, or is there a grain of truth in it?' A Jeffrey Archer character in his play about a newspaper office said: 'Do you want the truth, or do you want the press release?' Simon Hoggart wrote in *The Guardian* on 22 April 1994, when there was confusion over whether D-Day should be commemorated or celebrated: 'All public relations men are crass because they do not want to understand public opinion, only how to manipulate it. Churchill would no more have asked a PR man to organise a public commemoration than he would have had the fellow who drained his cess pit serve dinner to his guests. But times have changed and now we have a government which contracts out its most sensitive judgements to the sleaziest profession of them all.'

It is hard to combat such vilification. Yet the same invective could be flung at QCs for putting the best case for their clients, or a business for fighting its own corner (should it say: 'Buy the other guy's product, it's better'?) Is PR doing something wrong in helping businesses to do well? The best thing, advises Peter Preston, editor of *The Guardian*, is not to worry about it. It is in the interests of public relations that responsible media should enquire, investigate and report. Passing their scrutiny is a form of values auditing. Preparing management for that scrutiny is not only a matter of presentation (and what's wrong with that?) Poor presentation, poor public relations, get vilified by the media too. But perhaps that will open management's eyes to how they need to change.

If you are reading this book because you want a career in PR rather than wishing to learn about it for use in a job you already have, you need to think about how you might get started. A worthwhile first step for sixth formers and students is to book in with the IPR to attend their annual Careers Day, held in October. At the same time, ask them for a membership pack; that will bring you a miscellany of useful information. One or two of the IPR's regional groups put on a similar introductory event.

There are many reasons for studying public relations: for a better understanding of the discipline, to help you in your job, to give you extra skills as a manager, or to take it up as a career. The beauty of public relations is that it can be applied in whatever you do.

Having absorbed some of the information and ideas in this book you can follow up by reading more assiduously in areas that interest you. Studying any aspect of public relations can only improve your ability to do your job. For managers it is becoming a necessary part of their day-to-day armoury. Public libraries now stock a small range of books on public relations and the business shelves of good bookshops usually have at least half-a-dozen or so. Many excellent and seminal American texts are widely available. A list of books, and of organisations which can send you useful material, is at the end of this book.

Short courses

Half-day and day-long seminars and workshops are regularly available on most aspects of public relations. A few organisations run longer courses once or twice a year.

IPR workshops in London, open to non-members, include these topics: Introduction to Public Relations, Writing for the Press, Getting it Right in Print and Production, Research and Evaluation, Crisis PR, Corporate Strategy and Public Relations, Management of Public Relations Programmes, Public Relations in the Marketing Mix, Public Relations in the City, Public Relations Strategy, Introduction to Media Relations, Consulting Skills in Public Relations Practice, Public Relations and the Law.

Several other organisations, including the Public Relations Consultants

Association, run short courses and the Henshall Centre has a series of courses that move round the regions.

NVQs

The National Council for Vocational Qualifications was set up in 1986 to create a national structure of on-the-job qualifications. It awards National Vocational Qualifications (NVQs) when you are assessed as able to do tasks and jobs to an agreed standard. The Council says that 'NVQs have removed the barrier to learning and qualifications. NVQs have no unnecessary entry requirements, no prescribed method of delivery, no time limits for achievement, and no age limits.'

The Public Relations Education Trust (PRET), supported by the IPR and the PRCA, has converted its training matrix (see page 205) to provide an NVQ system for public relations.

NVQs have five levels. The CAM Certificate will be at level 3 and the CAM Public Relations Diploma at Level 4. A PR qualification at level 5 still has to be devised but is expected to be equivalent to degree level.

Communication, Advertising and Marketing Foundation (CAM)

CAM was set up in 1978. It runs examinations in advertising, marketing, public relations, sales promotion and direct marketing, media, and research and behavioural studies. The CAM Certificate is a general qualification in all six disciplines. You take the CAM PR Diploma after you have passed the Certificate examinations. CAM runs the examinations but not the courses. These are approved by the bodies taking part and are widely available, part time and evening, around the country.

CAM is a popular way of studying for a public relations qualification as the courses can easily be fitted in with work and there is a distance learning programme.

PR consultancies

Some of the big public relations consultancies run their own training courses for graduates and other staff. Most have regular in-house training of some kind. Working in a consultancy allows you to learn from the work of others.

Distance learning courses

PRET offers a distance learning programme. Stirling University students graduated from its distance learning course in 1994 for the first time.

First degree university courses

No university courses in public relations were available until 1989 when Stirling University began a one-year post-graduate course. By 1994 there were several first degree university courses over three, or four, years in Bournemouth, Cardiff, Edinburgh, Leeds, Plymouth and Preston (see Appendices).

All university courses combine book-learning, working in groups on projects, lectures and job placements. Practical work is essential because knowing about the skills of PR is one thing, being able to use them and think on your feet while doing so is quite another. Information on the content of one of the university courses is given in Chapter 4.

Post-graduate courses

One-year post-graduate courses are offered in Dublin, Manchester and Stirling.

Students with degrees in the humanities, communications, media and psychology have, thinks Stirling lecturer Jacquie L'Etang, something of an advantage in coping with the breadth of academic disciplines in the course. These include philosophy, psychology, communications, media studies, management and marketing.

'While there is an element of training,' she says, 'our primary mission is educational and we really do try to push people intellectually. Students are often impatient to get on and "do" things and are a bit surprised at the heavy reading load.' An important part of the learning process is the ability to think laterally and critically, and to develop strong analytical skills which can be expressed in logical argument. PR students at Stirling produce about seven 2–3000-word case studies, research reports and campaign proposals, nine or ten press releases, and four or five feature articles in the first 12-week term.

There are workshops and training sessions in negotiation and assertion skills, group dynamics, and presentation skills; management and crisis management games; and a case study weekend. Some of what they learn is not applicable in an entry level PR job because Stirling see their students as the international managers and strategists of the future. They put heavy emphasis on evaluation and research, issues management, campaign planning, corporate affairs and public communication campaigns.

International public relations

The Watford campus of West Herts College runs an exchange programme with a Paris college as part of its diploma course in international public relations. The course is sponsored by the Public Relations Consultants Association. The teaching covers: print, design and writing for the media; video, photography and broadcasting; public relations theory and techniques; PR media and advertising; psychology; market research and international marketing; languages, law and management disciplines.

The exchange programme was worked out by Betty Dean and Yves Bomati of West Herts College and the Institut Supérieur d'Enseignement des Relations Publiques, Levallois-Perret. It combines practical work and cultural reciprocity in 'real time' within an academic environment. One week is spent in the UK and one in France, ending with a presentation 'pitch' in the language of the host country. Students learn to recognise, accept and overcome cultural differences and working practices.

Apart from the experience gained in presentation skills in a foreign language and making a 'pitch' to foreign clients, the students have to reinforce their interpersonal and organisation skills, work under stress and pressure, and forge working relationships with people from a different background and culture within a few hours. A typical programme looks at a client problem from both sides of the Channel and students develop a public relations plan to solve it. They have tackled, for example, fashion, pollution, the Channel Tunnel, town twinning and tourism.

Work at it

To find a starter job in PR is not easy. But at least there are no rules and there are numerous points of entry. The new NVQ system should, slowly, open up ways for those leaving school at 16 or 18 and going to their first jobs, by building up simple qualifications in work as a basis for PR. If you are unemployed there is nothing to stop you spending time learning about public relations skills. You will need some of them in the way you approach finding a job – which, after all, is nothing less than a public relations and marketing campaign for yourself. If you are in a job you can study PR in your spare time and practise aspects of it whenever you have the chance.

Because judgement, experience and a reasonable amount of brain power are needed, the public relations industry tends to recruit from graduates. Not graduates in PR necessarily, but in any subject. A specialist subject – law, engineering, health, science – is sometimes useful in practising PR, as is plain experience of a work sector.

An ability with languages is of increasing importance within the EU, even if English is the most common working language. Media studies qualifications, with their close links to public relations; politics and economics, with the grounding they give in two of today's current affairs specialities; even old-fashioned subjects like history and English literature: all have their worth in encouraging mental organisation and clarity of expression.

Freelance

If you have some of the skills of public relations, it is possible to set up on your own at quite an early age, if you can offer a speciality. In the practical world, if you have accomplished one task you will suddenly find you are able to do other similar ones. If in your private life you have successfully organised a coach trip, a competition, a petition, you may have the kind of mind and outlook that will be wanted in event organisation.

Once you can offer your own freelance service you will be able not only to use your technical skills – event organisation, say, or writing newsletters, helping with presentations, translating – you will automatically be into public relations and marketing thinking.

You will have to devise a public relations plan, on however small a scale, for your new business. And you will soon find yourself able to offer your clients PR advice and ideas outside the strict technical service you are giving. In short, you are thinking – What's the aim? What's the message? What's the strategy? What's the plan? What are the likely consequences? What ways of communicating will work best? Let's work out a time table. What new things does your experience of these activities mean you should be doing instead (revise the plan)? What's the result? What went right, wrong? What next?

That in miniature is what public relations thinking is, whether for yourself, your department, a small company or a multi-national.

About a quarter of the Institute of Public Relations' members are self-employed.

7.2   The PR marketplace

Although the principles are always the same in any PR work, you may find yourself happier and more effective in one sector than another. You will certainly do different work, depending upon the sector. The main sectors are:

City, investor and financial	Employee relations
Local government	International
Government affairs	Community relations
Corporate communications	Crisis management
Public affairs	Media relations
Industrial and commercial	Charity and voluntary
Consumer	organisations

The main divisions of PR work in terms of employer are:

In-house   In-house PR people work only for the products, services, ideologies and commitments of the organisation employing them, whether it is, for instance, a multi-national, a small business, a charity or voluntary organisation, a pressure group, a firm of lawyers, accountants or architects, or a trade association.

The public sector   Public bodies dedicated to one service, like the police and local government, have been shrinking in number with privatisation (electricity and water utilities for example).

Government Information Services   The GIS, including the COI (Central Office of Information), and the whole of the civil service network, do not see themselves as in public relations. They are concerned with providing information rather than persuading. However, most of what they do overlaps with individual PR skills and you should send for their information folder. It is important to know about their services – and they are an employer.

PR consultancies   There are several hundred PR consultancies in the UK. They specialise in various skills and services which they offer for an annual fee, by the project, or for a retainer and an hourly charge.

The broad types of service offered by PR consultancies group like this:

- *Knowledge of a business or work sector* Because hiring someone who 'knows our business' is a criterion for management, having specialist knowledge is important. Thus a route into the PR business can be through knowing one type of work inside out. Journalism was, of course, the first example; followed by knowledge of the City. Other examples are: tourism, travel and leisure; healthcare and fitness; food and drink; IT, high-tech, computers; retailing; fashion; local authority; consumer goods; the construction and property industries; off-shore; brewing; personal finance.

  Consultants looking for new business will home in on areas which need to discover what PR is about. Schools and hospitals are two recent candidates. In the 1970s and 1980s the severe restrictions on publicity for the professions were gradually removed. Absurdly, architects had been supposed to wait for the phone to ring; they could not, as their code of practice put it, 'tout for business'; only respond. Now there are hardly any restrictions on architects, lawyers, civil engineers or other professions. Even doctors' practices now put out glossy brochures.

- *Knowledge of the PR and communications suited to particular work sectors* The types of PR programme devised depend on the natures of the publics to be approached. What is appropriate for dealers may not work with MPs. Some industries function by trading hospitality; others welcome serious seminars and conferences. Consumer PR is usually brasher and more colourful than industrial PR. Even the way information is passed to the media can differ from sector to sector. A study of the highly simplified case studies in this book will give a feel for the ideas which tend to work in different sectors.

- *Specialised knowledge of procedures* This kind of expertise is usually fairly high-powered. It is most common in corporate and financial public relations (take-overs, flotations, share issues, privatisations), in handling crises (experience one crisis and you can help with others), and in government relations and lobbying. It comes with familiarity of either client or consultancy operations and is one of the reasons for movement of staff between in-house departments and consultancies. Any general sector of PR practice leads to the opportunity to repeat knowledge gained elsewhere.

- *The technical PR skills* This is knowing how to use a particular channel of communications, one of the parts making up a whole campaign. Some of these skills are discussed in this book. Mastering, or having good experience of any one of these skills can make you a prospective employee for an in-house department or a consultancy, or capable of setting up on your own. The list includes: video and audio visual; design; advertising; publications; publicity; sales promotion; writing; house journals, newspapers and newsletters; production; media relations; seminars and conferences; hospitality; exhibition stands; sponsorship; presentation training.

Personal qualities

In public relations, introverts and extroverts, the shy and the bombastic, leaders, followers and independent spirits, are all welcome. When you are given a list of qualities needed in public relations they are so numerous you wonder that such paragons can exist. Some of the characteristics are even contradictory. You rarely find ideas people good at attention to detail for instance. The real point is that any group of people working on a project should have the qualities between them. This is rather hard on independent PR consultants and freelancers – but life's a bitch.

Different types of people probably orientate to different types of PR. Some think themselves better suited to in-house work than consultancy. If you feel a need to identify with an employer and a culture which you can relate to, and have a reasonably constant theme running through your working life, then in-house is for you. If, on the other hand, you like relief from one type of work by being busy on several at the same time; if you like to be part of different teams, and to have more frequent scope to practise specific communication skills, you will enjoy consultancy work. You do not have to make final decisions, only to advise on them. Generally there will be more scope for promotion in a largish consultancy, more training available and more exposure to learning a variety of communication skills. Ideally, however, you need to have experience of both environments.

Some typical characteristics

- You need to be able to communicate. It's obvious, but if you can't, you are trying to get into the wrong business
- You should enjoy finding out, looking for new ideas, acquiring information which will make you more useful to yourself, employees, colleagues, customers, clients and employers

- You must be able to plan and organise efficiently. If you are not good at attention to detail, work with someone who is
- Be open and honest within the limits of your brief. But don't be stupid and don't be too trusting
- You have to have flexibility, be able to change direction quickly, be sanguine when your ideas are turned down, changed or poached. Rebound with more and always carry out what has been agreed
- You need good nerve for the sharp end of the action, to deal with tough people, to keep a clear head when the pressure is on. But there is plenty of room in the business for back-room workers (so that others can take the kudos). Confidence comes with knowledge and experience
- You need stamina. PR is not a nine-to-five job. Always put your home telephone number on the press release. And some of the best ideas come when you aren't consciously thinking about them.

7.3 Step-by-step experience

One way into PR is to obtain a job with a supporting role to a PR function. This is the job description of support staff for the Infopress consultancy:

- Day-to-day support of account executives to back up their work with clients
- Liaise with clients and the media under the direction of account executives
- Answer calls when they are away or busy, take and pass on messages, or act on them
- Answer the nightline promptly and cover reception when needed
- Understand word processing; be able to enter information, print out documents, create and print mailing lists, mail merging and distribution list processing. Ensure all documents follow the Quality Standards Manual
- Look after clients' computer accounts and do the filing
- Liaise with Production Department
- Operate electronic communication links including PIMS (distribution service), IFAX and other on-line services.

Could you do someone else's job? Here, to end with, are typical days spent in a PR consultancy by an account executive (who handles work for several clients or 'accounts') and by an account director, further up the promotional tree, who directs work on a group of accounts.

Sharon Murphy – Account Executive, Infopress

9 February 1994

9.30 Working on a new business pitch, so checked the lists of forthcoming special reports in the national newspapers. These provide obvious opportunities for clients to supply useful information on the topic covered or even to have a by-lined article accepted. But the information has to be top level. The special reports, on subjects like Multimedia, Office Technology and International Telecommunications, are supported by advertising (which, whether you like it or not, can have an influence). Am interrupted by a fax from BT which needs an answer; then return to reading up for the pitch and noting down ideas.

11.30 Spend the next hour or so making phone enquiries to conference organisers over possible speaker opportunities for British Nuclear Industry Forum (BNIF). Then I look at BT's comments on a draft article, and put in the amendments until 1.30 when I break for lunch.

2.15 Continue working on the article, redraft parts of it, discuss it with another account handler, rejig it and fax to BT. Forty minutes spent checking *Marketing* magazine (for the new business pitch) and 25 minutes on more phone calls about speaking opportunities.

5pm Now I spend time on other clients, reading the daily press cuttings on one, magazines for another and writing to a journalist about a third. Tidying up goes down as management time – 15 minutes – and I go home at 6.15.

10 February

9.15 Spend 15 minutes putting more ideas on the business pitch into the computer, read the post (more management time) and phone BT. Then a 35-minute meeting to discuss the 1994 PR strategy for BNIF, and it's back to redrafting the BT article and checking magazines and press cuttings before ringing up journalists to investigate forthcoming editorial features identified on our media alert. Spend five minutes proofing a letter to Sedgwick Special Risks (a client) and then do more reading and research for the new business pitch. Half an hour for lunch.

2pm More calls for conference organisers for BNIF, to check out a speaking opportunity in Cairo. Request further details and a speaker registration form. Discuss Sedgwick Special Risks costings and read more magazines and press cuttings.

3.30 Off to a meeting with Sedgwick. Back to the office by 5 pm and more work on that BT article. More comments; more redrafting. Leave at 6pm.

Simon Greenbury – Account Director, Infopress

9 February

8.30 Meet designer to discuss invitation for Roncraft Murder Mystery Mayhem launch – a fun and unique approach to encourage consumer journalists to attend. An hour and a half spent on the Tea Lady of the Year Awards for Wellcome over the award presentation to the winner, new business, and drafting a release for Roncraft regarding their new advertising campaign, liaison with *ME* magazine about Casio Watch, and creating ideas for new Casio G-SHOCK watches to be launched at the end of May.

12.0 More work on the new business project until 3.30, interrupted by 30 minutes on Roncraft murder mystery invitation and product release.

3.30 Follow up on media relations work for Management Charter Initiative (MCI); on research for the parents/ Wellcome healthcare seminar – an idea to run a seminar for parents in conjunction with *Parents* magazine; further liaison with Roncraft on approval of invitation design and copy; more MCI chasing of media over case studies.

10 February

8.0am Spent until 4pm at the Casio Keyboard convention at the Edwardian Hotel, Heathrow. Attended, on invitation of client, to gain a real feel for new keyboards. Information to be used for two releases on new keyboards to teenage and grey markets. Included lunch with the MD and group product manager.

4pm More work on new ideas for Wellcome on Calpol and Drapolene rash brands.

The PR Matrix

At the same time as university syllabuses for the study of public relations were being constructed, the Institute of Public Relations and the Public Relations Consultants Association (PRCA) were worrying about the suitability of this or that course. Their solution was to publish, through the Public Relations Education Trust (PRET), an education and training matrix. For this, the education committees of the IPR and PRCA worked out (for the first time) a sequence of knowledge and skills which professional practitioners should have at successive levels of their careers. Courses were then approved according to the way they fitted in with the different levels and sections of the matrix.

You can use the matrix yourself as a neat and efficient self-assessment and study guide. Its virtues are the way it begins at the beginning and works upwards, its highly specific detailing of what is required, and its practicality. The matrix has been converted into the PR profession's structure for the new National Vocational Qualifications (NVQs) and can be obtained from the IPR or PRCA.

——— APPENDICES ———

1 Courses approved by the Institute of Public Relations

CAM Diploma in Public Relations, Dip(PR)CAM
CAM Foundation, Abford House, 15 Wilton Road, London SW1V 1NJ.
Telephone 0171 828 7506. Courses available around the UK.

Bournemouth
CNAA BA (Hons) in Public Relations

Bournemouth University, Poole House, Talbot Campus, Fern Barrow,
Dorset BH12 5BB.
Telephone: 01202 595105 or 524111

Four-year undergraduate course with the third year spent on
placement.

Dublin
Diploma in Public Relations
Dublin Institute of Technology, Aungier Street, Dublin Z.
Telephone: 010 353 1478 5252

One-year postgraduate course with two to four weeks spent on placement after finals.

Edinburgh
CNAA BA in Communication

Napier University, 10 Colinton Road, Edinburgh EH10 5DT
Telephone: 0131 444 2266

Three-year undergraduate course with no placement year

Leeds
BA(Hons) in Public Relations
Leeds Metropolitan University, Queen Square House, Woodhouse
Lane, Leeds LS2 8AB. Telephone: 0532 832600, ext 4367.

Three- or four-year undergraduate course with the third year spent on placement in the four-year course.

Plymouth
BA (Hons) in Public Relations

College of St Mark and St John, Derriford Road, Plymouth PL6 8BH. Telephone: 01752 777188

Three-year undergraduate course with the second year spent on placement.

Stirling
School of Management, University of Stirling, Stirling FK9 4LA. Telephone: 01786 467380.

One-year postgraduate course with optional placements in March.

Watford
Watford/PRCA Diploma in International Public Relations

West Herts College, Watford Campus, Hempstead Road, Watford WD1 2EZ. Telephone: 01923 257500.

Manchester
MA in Public Relations

Manchester Metropolitan University, Aytoun Building, Manchester M1 3GH. Telephone: 0161 247 6050 or 2000

One-year postgraduate course with placements phased in.

Preston
Combined Honours Degree in Public Relations

Lancashire Business School, Department of Journalism, University of Central Lancashire, Preston PR1 2HE
Telephone: 01772 893730 or 201201

Three-year undergraduate course with placement.

2 Further reading

General

All about public relations, Roger Haywood, McGraw-Hill
Effective public relations (7th Edn), Scott Cutlip, Allen Center and Glen
  Broom, Prentice Hall

Effective corporate relations, edited by Norman A. Hart, McGraw-Hill.
The handbook of public relations and communications (US), edited by
    Philip Lesly, McGraw-Hill.
The essentials of public relations, Sam Black, Kogan Page.

Specific sectors of PR work

Case studies
IPR Sword of Excellence award winning entries: back issues of the *IPR
    Journal*, the Institute of Public Relations.
The public relations case book, edited by Alan Capper and Peter Cunard,
    Kogan Page.
International public relations case studies, edited by Sam Black, Kogan
    Page.
Public relations in practice, Danny Moss, Routledge.

Crises
Crisis management, Michael Regester, Hutchinson Business Books.
Preventing chaos in a crisis, Patrick Lagadec, McGraw-Hill.
The first 24-hours, Dieudonnée ten Berge, Basil Blackwell, Oxford.

City and Financial
The financial public relations handbook, Kenneth Andrew, Woodhead-
    Faulkner, Cambridge.
Financial public relations, edited by Pat Bowman and Richard Bing,
    Butterworth Heinemann, for the CAM Foundation.
Investor relations, Michael Regester and Neil Ryder, Hutchinson
    Business Books.
Investor relations, David Lake and John Graham, Euromoney Publi-
    cations and Dewe Rogerson.
The annual report, Jasper Grinling, Gower.

Corporate
A sense of mission, Andrew Campbell, Marion Devine, David Young,
    Economist Books, Hutchinson.
Visual and corporate identity (for educational bodies), Clive Keen and
    David Warner, HEIST Publications, Banbury.
Managing your reputation, Roger Haywood, McGraw-Hill.
The corporate image, Nicholas Ind, Kogan Page.
Company image and reality, David Bernstein, Holt, Rinehart & Win-
    ston, Eastbourne.

Corporate reputation: managing the new strategic asset, John Smythe, Colette Dorward and Jerome Reback, Century Business.
The good guide to corporate citizenship, Marie Jennings, Woodhead-Faulkner Director Books.
A communication audit handbook, Seymour Hamilton, Pitman.

Internal
People, communication and organisations, Desmond W. Evans, Pitman.

International
International public relations in practice, edited by Margaret Nally, Kogan Page, London.

Lobbying and public affairs
Parliamentary lobbying, Nigel Ellis, Heinemann, for the CAM Foundation.
Right to be heard, Ian Greer, Ian Greer Associates, London.
Presenting your case to Europe, Peter Danton de Rouffignac, Mercury Business Books.
Pressure: the A–Z of campaigning in Britain, Des Wilson, Heinemann Educational.

Local government
Public relations in local government, Tom Richardson, Heinemann Professional Publishing, published for the CAM foundation.
Public relations for local government, Dick Fedorcio, Peter Heaton and Kevin Madden, Longman.

Management
How to understand and manage public relations, Dr Jon White, Business Books.
How to manage public relations, Norman Stone, McGraw-Hill.

Periodicals
PR Week (weekly)
PR Journal (monthly professional journal)
Public Relations Review (US quarterly), Connecticut.

Knowledge and skills

Communication studies
Introduction to communication studies, John Fiske, Methuen.
Communication theories, Werner J. Severin with James W. Tankard Jr, Longman.

Editing
BAIE editors handbook, British Association of Industrial Editors (Communicators in Business), Sevenoaks, Kent.

Exhibitions
Making the most of exhibitions, David Waterhouse, Gower.
Successful exhibiting, James W. Dudley, Kogan Page.

Examinations
Public relations revision workbook, Sam Black, HLT Publications.

Ideas
Managing ideas for profit: the creative gap, Simon Majaro, McGraw-Hill.

Marketing
Marketing communications, P.R. Smith, Kogan Page.

Market research
The industrial market research handbook, Paul Hague, Kogan Page.
How to do marketing research, Paul Hague and Peter Jackson, Kogan Page.

Media relations
Hitting the headlines, Stephen White, Peter Evans, Chris Mihill, Maryon Tysoe, The British Psychological Society, Leicester.
Surviving the media jungle, Dina Ross, Pitman.
Your message and the media, Linda Fairbrother, Nicholas Brealey Publishing.

Negotiation
The language of negotiation, Joan Mulholland, Routledge.
Negotiate, Willem Mastenbroek, Basil Blackwell, Oxford.

Personal communications skills
Putting it across, Angela Heylin, Michael Joseph.

The handbook of communication skills, Bernice Hurst, Kogan Page.

Presentation
How to handle media interviews, Andrew Boyd, Mercury.
Making an impact, Harvey Thomas and Liz Gill, David & Charles.
Media interview techniques, Peter Tidman and H. Lloyd Slater, McGraw-Hill.

Psychology
Consumer behavior, Prentice-Hall International, London.
Introduction to psychology, Harcourt Brace Jovanovich.

Sponsorship
Sponsorship, endorsement and merchandising, Richard Bagehot and Graeme Nuttall, Waterlow.
Successful sponsorship, Victor Head, Director Books.
How to get sponsorship, Stuart Turner, Kogan Page.
Hollis sponsorship and donations year book, Sunbury-on-Thames.

Theories
Organisational communication, Gary L. Kreps, Longman.
Excellence in public relations and communications management, edited by James E. Grunig, Lawrence Erlbaum.

Some reference books, media lists and support services to PR

Hollis press and public relations annual
(PR contacts in organisations, official and public information sources, PR consultancies, general reference and research addresses, services and suppliers for PR, sponsorship lists.)

Hollis Europe
(European public relations consultancies and networks; large European companies; information sources.)

The white book, Birdhurst Ltd, Staines.
(Production directory listing: agents and artistes; services and equipment for the entertainment, record, concert, film, conference and exhibition industries.)

Pocket pal, International Paper Company, Memphis.
(Graphic arts, print and production handbook)

Advance, Themetree, Aylesbury
(Advance notice of features, exhibitions and conferences.)

Benn's media directory, Tonbridge, Kent.

Blue book of British broadcasting, Tellex Monitors, London.

Editors, The Romeike Group, London.

Guide to European media, Grice Wheeler, Wimbish, Essex.

PR planner (UK) and *PR planner Europe*, Romeike Group
(Regularly updated loose leaf references to addresses for press, radio
and television; also on disk.)

PIMS, London
(Range of media directories; business, investor and government
relations directory; press release distribution; press cutting service.)

The media guide, edited by Steve Peak, A Guardian Book.

Two-Ten Communications, London
(Media directories including investment research analysts; feature writ
ing; media training.)

Press cuttings services include: Durrants Press Cuttings, International
Press-cutting Bureau, PIMS, Romeike Group.

Advertising in the media

BRAD – British Rate and Data, Maclean Hunter.

Willings press guide, Reed Information Service, East Grinstead.

3   PR organisations

The Institute of Public Relations (IPR)
The Old Trading House
15 Northburgh Street
London EC1V 0PR
0171-253 5151

The IPR, established in 1948, is the professional body for those engaged in public relations practice in the United Kingdom, and represents individual practitioners. It has 5000 members, all regulated by the IPR's Code of Professional Conduct. The institute has regional, vocational and special interest groups. Specialisations include: City and financial, government affairs, local government, internal communication, marketing communication, psychology, construction, engineering and technical, voluntary organisations and charities, health and medical, and tourism and leisure.

The IPR publishes guidelines on public relations work: public relations practice: its role and parameters; resolving the advertising/editorial conflict (about advertorials); PR and the law; fees and methods of charging for public relations services; the use and misuse of embargoes.

The IPR runs a series of workshops every year (see page 194).

Public Relations Consultants Association (PRCA)
Willow House
Willow Place
London SW1P 1JH
0171-223 6026

The PRCA represents its public relations consultancy members. It publishes the annual *Public relations year book*, listing its members and their clients (available in libraries).

The PRCA publishes guidance papers on public relations work: running an in-house training session; understanding public relations; client liaison; what is news; writing skills; guide to sponsorship; how to set up a royal visit; presentation skills; contingency planning; how to lobby in Britain; get it on air; media conferences; market research; planning corporate brochures; planning public relations programmes; consumer public relations; public affairs; corporate communications; PR for the high technology industries; international public relations; presenting press material; evaluating public relations activity; business to business public relations.

Confédération Européenne des Relations Publiques (CERP)
51 Rue de Verdun
F92158 SURESNES
Cedex
Paris, France
Fax: 33(1) 46 97 20 10

CERP was set up in 1959 to harmonise professional public relations practice throughout Europe and is now a confederation of 24 national public relations associations in 22 countries; their individual members are automatically members of CERP. It has consultative status with the Council of Europe, is recognised by UNESCO and is recognised and consulted by the European Union. CERP's codes of practice are the Code of Athens and the Code of Lisbon.

International Public Relations Association (IPRA)
Case Postale 1200
CH-1211 Geneva 2
Switzerland
22 791 0050

IPRA was formed in 1954 and has 1000 members in 64 different countries, offering networking opportunities to practitioners of at least five years' experience whose work has an international dimension.

Every three years IPRA holds a world congress. It has published nine Gold Paper studies on public relations: *Ethics* (1973 and 1991), *Education* (1976, 1982 and 1990), *Research* (1979), *The Communicative Society* (1985), *Propaganda* (1988), *The Environment* (1993), and *Quality* (1994).

Public Relations Education Trust (PRET)

PRET is jointly organised by the IPR and PRCA to further public relations education. In the autumn of 1994 it revised the IPR/PRCA Training Matrix (the criterion by which PR courses are approved) to match National Vocational Qualification (NVQ) needs, and it has developed a distance learning programme.

Public Relations Educators' Forum (PREF)

c/o The College of St Mark & St John
Derriford Road
Plymouth
Devon PL6 8BH

PREF is the organisation for the British public relations teaching profession and exchanges ideas on public relations education.

INDEX